SOCRATES AND JESUS

A DIALOGUE IN HEAVEN

SOCRATES AND JESUS

A DIALOGUE IN HEAVEN

Pierre Grimes Ph.D.

Introduction by Jeffrey Mishlove, Ph.D.

Socrates and Jesus: A Dialogue in Heaven

For information about this title or to order other books and/or electronic media, contact the publisher:

Opening Mind Press
OpeningMindPress.com
openingmindpress@gmail.com

ISBN: 979-8-9876413-0-9 (softcover)

Printed in the United States of America

Cover and Interior design: 1106 Design

Contents

Forevvord One

By Maria & Juan Balboa
Translators of Plato's Parmenides
Logos, Ana-Logos, Anti-logos

On the one hand, in Socrates we find The Paradigm of The Logos; for Socrates was, or better yet, Is, The Living Heart of Reason/Logos, whereas on the other hand, Jesus is said to be The Logos; The Masculine Offspring of The One God: For what is more Akin to Mind/Intellect than Reason, Truth, Light and The Way of Friendship that They Foster?

Furthermore Intellect/Mind: The Creator and The Soul: His Creation are Harmoniously In-Tune with Each Other by means of The Likeness that is Brought to Light by means of Analogy.

Then there is the body which stands opposite to Mind by being bereft of any Logos in-itself, but yet it is brought into Harmony with Mind by means of The Logos which the body acquires by means of the Soul, and thereby, The Christ/Logos Body becomes Incarnate Beauty by means of acquiring The Logos.

On the one hand, such also is The Harmony that is described by Dr. Grimes between the two Kindred Souls of Socrates and Jesus. Whereas on the other hand, so also is the anti-logos: the irrational indoctrinations of Aristotle and Saul/Paul of Tarsus, brought to light by Dr. Grimes. For their doctrines deny the validity and existence of Intellective Insights into the Very Nature of Reality, such as this one, that Plotinus often Participated of:

> "It has happened often. Roused into Myself from my body—outside everything else and Inside Myself—my gaze has met a Beauty Wondrous and Great.
>
> At such moments I have been certain that mine was the Better Part, mine The Best of Lives Lived to The Fullest, mine Identity with The Divine.
>
> Fixed There, firmly poised Above everything in The Intellectual that is Less than The Highest, Utter Actuality was mine.
>
> But then there has come the descent, down from Intellection to the discourse of Reason. And it leaves me puzzled. Why the descent?"
>
> —ENNEAD IV,
> 8–6 ELMER O'BRIAN TRANSLATION

Aristotle and Paul produced their so called teachings as if they were of more importance than those of their Masters. However, later on; when the Platonists saw that their era was drawing to a close, they reintroduced Perennial Philosophy (and as such, takes root and blooms in any soil) in the very Just guise of Dionysius the Areopagite: the follower of Paul of Tarsus; since the Platonists perceived this inequality and lack of Harmony and they desired to bring others to the Harmonious and Higher teachings of their Masters.

Now we take another quote, this time from the poem of Parmenides as an example of the journey humans can take in order to come to know The Calm Heart of Well-rounded Truth.

"The Goddess then received me with Willing-Mind, and taking my hand in Her Right hand, then proclaimed the following Oracular Speech to me: O Prepared-Youth, joined with Immortal Charioteers and worthy mares that bring you to Our Abode! Welcome!

Seeing that it is No evil fate that has Pre-escorted you back again upon this Journey (For It is that which exists outside of the beaten-paths of men), but Law/Custom/Order and Justice.

Thus, it is Necessary, that you enquire into All subjects: on the one hand, The Unshaken/Calm Heart of Well-rounded Truth, and on the other, the opinions of mortal human-beings, in which there exists no right opinion.

For it is Necessary, that you should nevertheless learn this also, so that the appearances be tested: through all ways from every side, just as they are." Fragment 1
—Balboa translation

Dr. Grimes is a Master at guiding others on this journey of discovery through the use of Dreams and Philosophical Midwifery and Philosophical Insight; which is evident in his dialogue between Socrates and Jesus. We invite you to join in this journey through your own exploration of this work.
—January 2015

Foreword Two

I was just finishing up my graduate work in philosophy at Holy Apostles College and Seminary when I first discovered the work of Pierre Grimes. My days had been spent immersed in a deep reading of Plato's *Republic* for a seminar, and I was so enthralled by Plato's conception of the soul that I wanted to remain immersed in the little-known world of Platonic spirituality even after I just couldn't force myself to read anymore. So late at night I searched for lectures on YouTube, found an enormous collection of Pierre's talks—and systematically watched every last one of them over the next few months.

Stunned to find a living exemplar of the Platonic tradition, which I had thought must have either died out long ago with Thomas Taylor—or become merely de-Paganized, certain of its features absorbed into Christianity—I became more and more captivated as I discovered not only that Pierre was a living thread in this profound tradition but that he had enlivened and greatly expanded it with insights from Eastern spiritual traditions and Western psychology. Far more than that, Pierre has actually founded an entire school of philosophical psychology known as Philosophical Midwifery, built around Plato's insights into mistaken ideas about the Self. I felt that I had stumbled onto a treasure trove. For sure I had found something I'd never really had before—an intellectual mentor.

I was at the time a strictly conventional Catholic believer. I had chosen my graduate program specifically because it rigorously adhered to the Magisterium of the Church (the Church's teaching office). My main research interest was the Platonic vein that ran through the Church's intellectual history from Thomas Aquinas to Augustine and right back to the Prologue of St. John. So although a deep interest in Platonism had led me to Pierre's thought, I was initially very dismissive of his talks that called into question the commonplace understanding of the message and character of the Gospels, and especially the figure of Jesus. I was adequately familiar with the major claims of New Testament scholarship and how they threw into doubt certain central dogmatic teachings about Jesus, but my commitment to Catholic orthodoxy was so strong that I couldn't even see what was there to be seen in the texts, to put it as Pierre often does.

Even in his late 90s, Pierre maintains a strong online presence so, on a lark, I sent him a note telling him how much I had come to value his work. To my surprise, he wrote back and offered to meet me in Sedona, Arizona, a couple hours north of me, for a cup of coffee and a talk. I was thrilled, and a short while later I was sitting in a café with this man who would be considered a true sage at any point in history.

Anyone who knows Pierre will agree that he is thoroughly humble despite his monumental intellectual achievements and spiritual attainment, and boundlessly generous with his time, attention, and knowledge. In the way of all great teachers, he patiently answered all my many questions in a manner that, in a few simple words, produced realization even about the most abstruse matters. During the course of our many talks over the next couple of years, the conversation would turn often to Pierre's interest in the figure of Jesus as revealed by recent New Testament scholarship, a topic that always made me just a bit uneasy because I knew it probably threatened my strict orthodoxy. I say "probably" because I had always experienced cognitive dissonance in reading the New Testament; it was obvious at some more or less conscious level that the gospel accounts did not cohere with one another, that Paul was in conflict with James and even Jesus, and that, perhaps most importantly, Jesus' actual words, insofar as we can guess what they were likely to have been, were clearly not unambiguously the foundation, or even always much of a concern, for large sections of mainstream Christianity. Like so many of my fellow Christians, I suffered from a kind of insecurity about my theological commitments that, in discussions with others, would express itself in hand-waving assurance that, somehow, at a higher level, such conflicts could be overcome—or even at times in outright hostility.

Nonetheless, when Pierre offered me the tremendous honor of editing *Socrates and Jesus*, and helping to bring it to press, I could hardly have said no to the opportunity to wander in the garden of these ideas, which his conversation had made for the first time genuinely interesting to me.

This led to a personal odyssey that took me through an exploration of the trajectory of the historical development of the figure of Jesus, a development that begins with the mysterious unconventional rabbi teaching about the way to the experience of the "kingdom of heaven," to the later claim that he was the awaited Jewish messiah and in some obscure sense the "son of God," all the way to the formal declaration at the council of Nicaea that he is the second person of a triune godhead through whose death and resurrection alone it is possible to avoid eternal damnation. This was a movement that would take Christianity from being a religion *of* the teachings of Jesus and the state of mind he taught was necessary to enter the inner "kingdom" to being a religion *about* Jesus, where emphasis is placed on accepting a set of beliefs that mark one's belonging to a community. The sense of estrangement may then be overcome, but, as Pierre would say, the "believer" lacks *ousia*: the inner self-reflective power that leads to spiritual self-realization, the ultimate aim of this human existence.

As emerges in the course of the dialogue, the pivotal figure in this redirection of the understanding of Jesus is Paul of Tarsus, Jesus' most important interpreter insofar as mainstream Christian doctrine is largely drawn from his letters. Look to the *Catechism of the Catholic Church*, to Luther's *Catechism*, or to the Christology of any mainline Christian denomination, and you will find that it is almost all taken from Paul's letters and not from Jesus' actual teachings (or what scholarship tells us is likely to have been his teachings). For Pierre, interpreters of those who, like Jesus or Socrates, bring forward a new teaching, fall into five classes, and Paul is of the third: those who posture as accepting the new teaching while in reality replacing the new system with one of their own. That something like this happened in the case of Paul seems pretty well established by New Testament scholarship and not hard to see even from a layperson's unbiased reading of the texts either.

Just take a simple example. Mark 10:17–28 tells the story of the Rich Young Ruler. The young man runs up to Jesus, kneels before him, and asks, "Good Master, what shall I do that I may inherit eternal life?" His question, of course, is about "salvation," which is a major point of contention among the many Christian sects. Is it attained through grace? Election? Faith alone? Faith plus works? Here, Jesus is being asked *point-blank* how it is we come to be "saved," and one would think that for this reason his answer would be the centerpiece of Christianity. But it is not. Instead, what scriptural passage comes to mind for most Christians when asked about salvation? Probably one like Romans 10:9, which says that "if you declare with your mouth, 'Jesus is Lord,' and believe in your heart that God raised him from the dead, you will be saved." If this was Jesus' teaching, why in the world wouldn't he have used the Rich Young Ruler's question as an opportunity to have set it forth for the benefit of the world? Instead, Jesus replies that salvation is attained through following the law and, as his later instructions will make clear, not just externally but with *understanding*. Paul's teaching and that of Jesus are, to me, plainly different and irreconcilable except through the often tortured logic of Christian exegesis. This conflict between Paul and the Jesus of Mark is, as Jesus points out in the dialogue, surprisingly systematic: ". . . what Paul put in his account is not in Mark, and what Mark said, Paul ignores completely," an observation that I find confirmed in my own studies.

And what is it that Pauline theology is a substitute for? Ignoring Jesus' ministry, Paul sought to form a worldwide network of churches anchored in a doctrine ("substitutionary atonement") that was both a belief system and a belonging system. Jesus became the scape-goat that allows believers to escape from their sense of guilt while assenting to a belief system that brings a sense of community and belonging, thereby overcoming estrangement. But, because it is accepted through "faith" and not understanding, it often precludes the self-examination and reflection that leads to spiritual realization. The believer becomes more comfortable in the ego as well as more entrenched in the ego instead of transcending it—instead of coming to the experience of the Kingdom of God that is already in our midst (Luke 17:21). Strangely enough, a reading of the Synoptic Gospels, which tend to be most in opposition to Paul, reveals a Jesus who is preaching the *opposite* of scapegoating—the opposite of offloading one's sins onto a sacrificial victim. His disciples are responsible for attaining the understanding that leads to the Kingdom (Mark 12:34); they're not shoe-ins just because they confessed a creed or received a sacrament. Among many other ignored precepts, those who would take him as their spiritual master must also learn to love God with their whole being and their neighbor as themselves. I have often thought Christians, like me, should dwell on these two "Greatest Commandments" and not move on to anything else until they can be said to actually realize them in the heart. Just think: what would it mean to love the divine with all one's heart or to really love your neighbor as yourself? If we did simply this, we would be Bodhisattvas, Sadhus, and great Saints.

Stripped of what are likely to be, and in many cases assuredly are, later theological accretions, we find Jesus as a great spiritual personality with a teaching surprisingly similar to that of Socrates. As Pierre points out, there may have been a geographical reason for this, but also and more fundamentally, both Socrates and Jesus are expressions of what has been called the Perennial Philosophy, which stands behind all the world's great wisdom traditions. As Pierre says, Socrates' account of this essential philosophical foundation of all past cultures is beautifully presented in terms of his central analogy, that the Good or the One is to the Most Brilliant Light of Being—alternatively called the Idea of the Good, Intellect, Nous, or Logos—as the Idea of the Good is to Helios, or the Sun. Meditation on this analogy reveals that the Logos is both within and without, and that it is possible because of this kinship for the human being to participate in the life of the Good. In the traditional metaphysics Socrates represents, the Most Brilliant Light of Being or Logos can truly be said to be the Son of God, the presence of the divine in our experience, and the basis of spiritual love. This profound, transformative teaching is buried in later interpretation, just as Jesus' teaching was. The astonishing similarities between Socrates and Jesus, both in terms of their core message as well as in relation to Socrates' question, "What has happened to the gifts we left man?" is, as far as I know, an insight original to Pierre.

It is in light of this common ground between these two great figures that I have come to encounter Jesus for the first time, to put it in Christian terms, and gain a vastly enriching perspective on the teachings of Socrates as well. This is a book that not only offers countless suggestive ideas for curious readers to follow up on; it is a work to be meditated on and that will challenge and perhaps change your perspective. *Socrates and Jesus* is an invitation to a rediscovery of these two foundational figures as well as an excellent introduction to the thought of the incomparable Pierre Grimes.

– **Doran Hunter**
Buckeye, Arizona, July 18th, 2020

Introduction

JEFFREY MISHLOVE, PH.D.

Before reading Pierre Grime's brilliant manuscript,
I had imagined that a conversation in the afterlife between Jesus
and Socrates might reveal two very different personalities at odds
with each other. I was pleasantly surprised, however, to discover
that former U.S. President George W. Bush may have been onto
something when he referred to Jesus as his favorite philosopher. For
Pierre has revealed the philosophical basis underlying the actual
teachings of the original Nazarene. How similar are the teachings
of Jesus and Socrates to each other? What are their differences? In
Pierre's presentation, the similarities between Jesus and Socrates
are stronger than I had imagined. One might even say that Jesus
was actually a philosopher.

Is it possible, after more than two thousand years, for us to
know what either Jesus or Socrates really taught? Perhaps not. But
it makes sense to study the different interpreters of these men carefully and to notice the differences between them. This is precisely
what Pierre has done.

Are the different presentations of the teachings of Jesus and
of Socrates in basic agreement concerning the main ideas of each
individual? Pierre points out that, in the case of Jesus, there is a clear

demarcation between the teachings of Paul and those of Jesus as found in the Nag Hammadi texts (as well as in some of the Gospels). How similar are the teachings of Jesus and the contemporary practice of Christianity? Pierre suggests that the Pauline doctrines of Christianity are antithetical to the actual teaching of Jesus.

What does it mean to die in order to save others from their sins? Pierre argues that it is not helpful to protect others from the consequences of their own behavior. He prefers a philosophical approach wherein one comes to understand and even make amends for one's mistakes.

How does Gnostic Christianity relate to these traditions? Gnostic Christianity emphasizes the ability of the individual to achieve gnosis. In that sense, it is akin to the goal of enlightenment in Eastern religions. It is also akin to the Socratic ideal often expressed as "Know Thyself."

What are the practices that Jesus and Socrates each recommend? Pierre suggests that the practice most recommended by Jesus himself was the careful study of his biblical parables. There are about thirty of them. What are the roles of analogy and allegory in the teachings of Socrates and Jesus? Pierre argues that the parables of Jesus are critical to an understanding of his teachings. But these are rarely emphasized in Christian religious practice. Socrates, of course, makes ample use of similar analogies and allegories—such as the famous allegory of the cave.

From Socrates, Pierre derives a practice of paying attention to dreams. What role do dreams play in religion and in philosophy? Pierre argues that both philosophy and religion have either ignored or downplayed their crucial importance.

How similar are the Hellenic and the Judaic traditions? To what extent have they influenced each other? Judaism, Christianity, and Hellenism have been intertwined for centuries. It is fair to say that, despite their differences, they are intimately interwoven with each other. How similar are the teachings of Socrates and the contemporary practice of philosophy? Philosophy today has moved very far away from the Socratic dictum of "Know Thyself."

How do Jesus and Socrates each relate to the notion of divine illumination? This notion is central to the teachings of both individuals.

– Jeffrey Mishlove
Host, *New Thinking Allowed* YouTube channel

Socrates and Jesus
A Dialogue in Heaven

By Pierre Grimes

Among the rolling hills north of here there is a meadow where souls of those who have recently died meet and discuss their former life on Earth. It is here that they greet those souls coming down from Heaven and up from the House of Hades. After they greet old friends and relatives, tears flow and laughter follows as they share their stories. Then, they settle down for the presentation of a play that is not a play. It continuously plays from the beginning for each soul. It can be stopped and started any time a soul wishes to pause and reflect upon any part of this strange play. Even before the play unfolds, opposing voices are heard that raise troubling doubts and deep concerns about the ideas presented in the play itself.

CHORUS

Another showing of this empty play is about to begin. I'll tell you that whatever is said will never get you anywhere. How can anyone claim to speak for Socrates or Jesus? On the face of it, it is arrogantly presumptuous. A dialogue with these two is as improbable as it is impossible. It's going to be as foolish as it will be absurd. There are so many interpreters who claim they speak the truth; the roars of

I

these conflicting voices drown one another out. How can anyone find a single voice amidst all these voices that is true above all the others? These voices may appear sometimes to share something, but their differences are what confuse us true believers.

Once you have heard the voice of Jerusalem, who needs the empty chatter from Athens? You may not be able to escape, but we can warn you that nothing worthwhile can follow. The best of words is a hollow echo of man's stupidity in trying to comprehend the incomprehensible. Man can never understand his own folly because of his own inherent ignorance.

Anti-Chorus

Put aside your desire to escape and see if there really is something here for you. Let's wait and see what is yet to be said. You believe nothing will come of this, don't you? I'll tell you that everything you will hear discussed right here can turn you around to ponder something truly astonishing.

So just watch how the symphony of words can overcome your chorus of dissonant voices. Awaken your curiosity and you'll see how well-placed words can dispel your confusion. Perhaps behind your desire to flee you are afraid of what new fear may come from all this. Could your worry conceal your fear of the mind?

Socrates

It is good that we could come together to explore some ideas. The question we were given was, "What has happened to the gifts we left man?" Surely Providence has brought us together and even now she might be somewhere listening to what we say.

Jesus

Yes, the divine moves in profound ways and has finally brought us together to answer that very question. While it is curious that we have been asked to do this, there is no ignoring that request. You have engaged in many skillful explorations in your dialogues; why not go ahead and lead this one? I'll follow along and I'll pick up your style of dialoguing as we go.

SOCRATES

Is it likely that you are no stranger to Hellenic thought? I ask that because from what I have heard, you lived rather close to the center of Stoic thought, and you also speak Greek, do you not?

JESUS

Yes, that is true. I was born in Nazareth in Galilee, which was part of a culture that was deeply influenced by Hellenism. We had three hundred years of Hellenic influence, and we were bilingual, with the Greek language playing a key role throughout the entire region. Galilee, by the way, had no capital and, most curious to some, only one small synagogue at Magdala. The center of Stoic and Cynic philosophy was only a day's walk from where I was born. Those philosophers were living their teachings. Their philosophical systems have much in common with what has been attributed to my teachings. However, neither of these schools of philosophy ever attempted to create a Church system. They were content to express their own thought as a way of life rather than as a way of belief.

SOCRATES

Once again I see that there is a greater depth behind your life and teachings than I had imagined. Did you know that we call Stoic and Cynic philosophers Platonic? They came after me and did their own interpreting. They are without metaphysics, mythology, or dream work, yet, for all that, they are still part of our spiritual tradition.

It was during those times that some philosophers took on the
name Cynic, but that name, of course, in Greek, means dog, and
was used by the populace as an abusive and derogatory term. It was
also at that time that philosophers were driven underground by the
oppressive forces of society. As a result, some became secretive, and
their teachings became esoteric. Did you get into these philosophers?
And what of your interpreters?

Jesus

Yes, I did know that. Did you believe that there could be a center
of these philosophers living so close and I ignored what is central
to me? Before we decide on the meaning of my works, you have to
decide who speaks for me. Most have a popular view of my mission
drawn from what are called the gospels; they include Mark, Matthew,
Luke, and John. Apart from these, there are also the teachings of
Paul. There is no harmony among these works. There is another
set of gospels called the Gnostic Four, and they need to be explored
and looked at before you decide what my teachings are. It did not
stop with them since later interpreters went on for many years to
create their own version of my sacred work.

Socrates

I am pleased we cleared up that point. Now, the struggle over
who could speak for you must have been a lively one. We will need
your reflections upon this if we are to understand why your teachings
fragmented into these clashing groups.

Jesus

Doubtless your followers were equally clashing with one another
as they likely are even now. I have heard that while you have continued
your dialogues even here, there are widely different interpretations of
them. I'll trade you my reflections for those you had with your group.

Socrates

True it is, and since my departure from Earth I have been in dialogues here with Orpheus, Musaios, and both Homer and Hesiod. And then there is Palamedes; you doubtless know of his curious exploits and his divine counterpart.

Jesus

You say your group included Orpheus and his son, Musaios; surely that is a wondrous group. I do know of Orpheus as the first prophet among your people, the founder of your theology, and he brought your people to understand the symbols that unlock the mysteries. I have heard his oracles covered much, and he left your people with the vision of the ages, didn't he?

Socrates

You ask a question from a background I couldn't even guess you had. Then, with a smile, you drop in something I had not heard about. What is this vision of the ages that you mentioned just now?

Jesus

It should not surprise you that I have known about the prophets and theology because theology is the study of the nature of the divine. I learned of this vision from sages I have encountered here, just as you have encountered sages in your group. I recently spoke to one who described in mighty words that man's condition is that he is emerging from ignorance and reaching for that intelligible light that brings to birth a kind of understanding that benefits its beholder.

Socrates

Indeed, as I listen to your words, I see I have found another person I can reflect with who will awaken what I most want to grasp. So please share with me this vision that sounds, indeed, as if it came from Orpheus.

JESUS

From what I have learned, the vision was originally sculpted in stone and placed at the entrance to the Temple of Apollo in Thrace. It said that at first mankind was without the words to understand himself, then with the dawn of language came the age of sages and prophets, and this was followed by the eclipse of that light, and finally its restoration came with the dawn of the true man.

SOCRATES

Curiously enough, at our group's last talk, as we discussed not only the power of ignorance and its terrible grip upon man, we also explored the nature of Wisdom and sought to discover if it has the power to overcome the worst effects of ignorance. The only popular remedy that was put forward by most was to become initiated into the Eleusinian mysteries, and most agreed that the failure to become initiated kept one in a state of mind we call ignorance.

JESUS

I expected you would add that you philosophers cultivate memory to become more perfect. I notice that your group didn't explore the nature of sin, but rather the power of the presence or the absence of Wisdom.

SOCRATES

You are correct there, Jesus. After exploring the extremes, the mean should be easier to unfold. With our questions we are likely to benefit, and it might even give us a way to grasp the way Providence unfolds.

Jesus

You are right in that view. It is not often that we are a given the chance to see how Providence unfolds. Clearly, we have both continued your quest here in the heavens, as I have also been a participant in the divine luminosity. You refer to being in that state as being in the Isles of the Blest. As you know, the paths we travel along are parallel and are illuminated through the divine. As you were commanded to be a philosopher, so I was appointed to fulfill my sacred mission. Our teachings were directed at both common people and an inner circle. We both faced a fierce prejudice against our spiritual paths. You were accused, tried in public court, sentenced, and died for what you truly are, just as some say I too suffered that same fate. Further, our work has continued to flourish. Most important, we both experienced profound spiritual states that shaped our lives and our teachings. It is from this sameness we can go along the path of comparing not only our teachings, but also the way our teachings have been passed on to others.

Socrates

True that is, Jesus, and we both saw the depth and power of that prejudice. It springs from a fear of the Mind. The fear drowns out any voice that seeks a rational approach to the encounter with the divine. I, too, have had followers who even denied it was possible to truly know the furthermost reach of the Mind. I went along an ancient path that others before me had taken, and surely others will follow after me. Those who seek that true knowing of the eternal and unchanging may even go beyond that to that which is beyond knowing. Yet it is also obvious that some among those who are called our followers deny the light and return to their own darkness. Curious, is it not, that what we bring, others are quick to deny? There are some who offer what we never said in order to conceal their fear of the light. While we explore our sameness, we should also turn our attention to those whose fear drives them to escape from the light.

Jesus

True, they run away from what we are drawn to. So, they either find a way to escape, or they are drawn to the same thing that we are drawn to. Are we so different from the rest of mankind that our teachings can't work on the many? They run away from the light and hide behind impossible beliefs. They adopt the most outrageous folly as if it were the highest Truth. They cultivate a kind of blinding ignorance that leaves no room for intelligible light.

Socrates

Is it true that we share many teachings and practices, or do we differ in the one and not the other?

Jesus

I do believe we share a similar public practice and that much of our teachings are similar, but not the same. We both seize upon those moments when we see people receptive and open to being challenged. At those times, we confront their most fundamental beliefs so that a new and more spiritual level of understanding can emerge. We both urge them to turn to that light that illumines all things and brings smiles to the wise. Our difference lies in that I challenge those in my circle to enter the Kingdom of God, while your circle is society itself, and you seek to bring your fellow man into that light. Further, your way, Socrates, I believe achieves the same goal but in different ways. You lay bare the shortcoming in men's behavior and in the reasoning they use to justify themselves. Your eye is always on the drama behind justice and injustice. You offer a way of reasoning that centers in the rational vision of man. By displaying before them an ideal way of reasoning, it brings them to a new vitalizing sense of truth. You urge excellence in all that is done. What is this but to bring that sense of excellence to their search for a more profound inner way of being? You urge contemplating Truth.

My work challenges my people's unthinking commitment to an apocalyptic vision and eschatology. For the true destiny of man is to be discovered here and now through self-discovery and not through the destruction of the Cosmos.

Socrates

You have expressed our similarity well, but I would highlight the issue of practice. You are correct to stress that each of us has a practice; however, my practice is so complete that it is my way of life. Still, I need to say that it is driven by my duty to God, for I have been chosen by God to fulfill the task of being a philosopher. There is no higher role or benefit than my acting out my role in Athens.

Jesus

Yes, we share that kind of practice, even though we went along different ways to achieve it. Surely I know you have tried to understand and deal with similar problems, Socrates, so how would you express what you found? However similar we may seem, our interpreters find differences most startling and extreme. Can there be a way to understand these many interpretations of what we have said and done? Is there something that drives this fragmentation of the Logos into irreconcilable parts?

Socrates

What I saw many times is that the return to the darkness of shadowy belief was simply because they believed their beliefs were clearer and truer than what we had shown them. Does taking on early beliefs make it too difficult to see what is here to be seen? Or shall it be said that the problems that are manifested during one's earthly existence can only be solved in the afterlife? Or does the fullest expression of problems experienced on Earth reveal what you need to see, but you must await death to see if the solutions of those problems truly benefit after death?

JESUS

Yes, Socrates, I do see why you came to those issues.

SOCRATES

I like the way we are reviewing this task of ours; however, it leaves me with another question. When you want to study anything that is a whole, should we not be careful that we start off identifying each of its parts? For surely any interpretation should treat each part, or piece, of the whole with integrity, or one's efforts will fail.

JESUS

Yes, that is a good way to go.

SOCRATES

Then, whatever interpretation is made of our work, it would be wise to judge if each interpretation gives a balanced and fair representation of the whole of which the parts are parts of our work, would you not agree?

JESUS

I can agree to that while still wondering about why there are so many interpretations of our work. Among my interpreters, I even wonder if there are some who came to see my own deepest thought about the divine destiny of man, but who have been rejected by the many.

SOCRATES

If you please, we could examine what each of these interpretations said about the destiny of man, couldn't we? Collecting these interpreters in terms of their likeness and unlikeness just might help us review them and judge if they have advanced our thought or not. These interpreters of ours may fit into a single category, or idea, and that raises an interesting question: Are there natural divisions or parts of that whole?

JESUS

I certainly am not against exploring any idea. However, I have often wondered if it is worth all the effort to break an idea into so many pieces. I wonder what benefit follows from chasing down their sameness or likeness in the idea of the destiny of man.

SOCRATES

As interesting as it might be to explore that idea, it would be different from the task we have been given.

JESUS

I agree with that. What do you offer?

SOCRATES

If our search requires us to examine many voices, would it not be interesting to see if there are only a finite number of interpretations so that their samenesses can be addressed? If so, it might reduce the vast number of voices to a finite set of groups and that will let us address each as we go. Shall we then review those presumed followers of ours to see how many groups or divisions they fall into? However, if it turns out that our interpreters do not fall into well-defined classes, we will be at a loss to understand what has been going on. I am one of those people who don't like to admit that there is no order in the realm of reasoning.

JESUS

Now I am for that idea. It may prove to be an interesting way of going. What is the source of that model you plan on following, Socrates? Or did you discover this approach yourself?

SOCRATES

It was Plato who said that Prometheus' gift to man was the dialectic. From that gift, all the arts came into existence that moved man from being a creature of nature that was forced to live in caves to being able to be a mean between Nature and the Intelligible realm. He taught us that before a subject is to be explored, it is important to first draw the divisions within that subject and then to see how they relate to one another. Then, from Hesiod and Aeschylus we learned much about Prometheus. Together they are the ones who carried the torch of reason that has helped us understand the human predicament. All mankind is caught between the extremes of being part of Nature and the Intelligible.

JESUS

Now, Socrates, as I might have expected, I see that means you are following through with the gift of Prometheus. I would still like to see if making these divisions helps us understand what lies behind this multiplicity of voices.

SOCRATES

Let's take this problem of ours and state it in the most general of terms. Then we will be able to see if it fits our particular problem.

Jesus

Yes, that is likely, and it just might also explain why this flood of interpreters war against one another. Perhaps, as we continue with this task of ours, it may help us understand our fundamental difference.

Socrates

Surely, and finding such a difference and making it clear should help us see what irreconcilable difference there is that cannot be bridged or brought into a unity.

Jesus

Then, as you consider these divisions of interpreters, would you please set forth what it is you have come to see about their necessity?

Socrates

Now, that is fair. We can say that whenever a new truth is brought into view, there are some who accept it in full as it is. In possessing their new vision, they drop the old and have little need to comment on the old. Next there are those who hear it and reject it totally because they have a fierce loyalty to the old and do not want to believe anything new. A third group gives the appearance of accepting the new, but in reality they substitute their own alien system for the new while claiming a higher truth guides their own creation. They subvert and deny the new while claiming to speak for it. Clearly their own core beliefs are so threatened that they claim they know the truth about the new and they craft their creation to replace the new. They switch one thing for another as if by magic and insist this is the new. We could call them wolves appearing as sheep.

Last, there are those who apply the new to support the weakness perceived in their old system of belief. These can be said to have a primary interest in saving their own primal core beliefs by putting patches on an old garment. Or we can say that this last group applies a metaphysical structure to their primal core beliefs to revitalize their old beliefs. We can say they rationalize their past system by finding analogies and parallels between the old and the new. We can say that they function intellectually to convert to reason systems that were non-rational or less rational. We could call them Hellenic saviors of the old through using the tools of reason.

However, let me be a bit cautious because I may need another division. For what if we find someone who doesn't fit in any of our groups?

Jesus

Well, I don't know about that last remark of yours, but if you need a fifth or even sixth, I shall be pleased to grant it. You chose a difficult path. For now, you will need your four, and maybe five explanations, instead of looking through the many for the single one that could eliminate all the others.

Socrates

You caught the purpose of this dialectic because identifying proper divisions within an idea makes visible the order behind the diversity, and this makes apparent the rational structure operating within ideas. If the divisions also admit of the development of stages within an idea, then it is possible to anticipate and understand the emergence of these divisions within a hierarchy.

Jesus

Surely that way of going does have advantages, because the seed of Truth will be flourishing along the way of our journey.

Socrates

Difficult it may be, and it may prove worthwhile to keep our minds open to new possibilities. It will also give us an opportunity to see if the way of the dialectic can uncover truths that might be too difficult to reach without it. Surely we both know that our task does present us with a challenge that just might bring to birth what we both love to see: Truth.

Jesus

Yes, Socrates, and to share such Truth with a lover of Truth is its own prized reward. The benefit you gained from your discussion with your sages here in Heaven is obvious. You have a history of sages; we have had prophets. Did you know that we have at least sixty-two Major Prophets, and of them seven were women?

Socrates

Yes, prophets played a vital role in your history, as did the sages in ours. However, as you consider them now, would you say your prophets escaped the charge of being innovators, or did they bring new beliefs to support their own core beliefs? Anytime a new idea enters society, the question always arises as to whether or not the new is truly true and can be reconciled with the old.

Jesus

Really, do you recall a ready test for the truth of a new idea? The test for the truth of these new ideas should be balanced by some test of the old to determine if they are true. Still, Socrates, I like the name you have given for the old and new. You call what are new those ideas that are new to a culture since they lacked them before. You call the old the traditions and beliefs of prophet belief systems.

SOCRATES

Sure thing, because we could reverse the terms and call the Hellenic traditions the old and the impact of Judaism upon the Hellenic tradition the new, couldn't we? However, since we are doing the first comparison it is not likely we will need the second. So, what do we have? Well, I would very much like to understand the struggle these belief systems have when they try to assimilate or reject the Logos of the sages.

JESUS

Yes, core beliefs play a major role in framing every thought of the believer. Judaism is many things and takes on many forms. The future shows its newer forms are shaped by history. The spirit of man always finds creative ways to express the divine. The core beliefs can be reflected and modified under the force of the new. Indeed, from the same divine vineyard, old and new wine come. However, for all the changes some are always there; so I would say your idea of fundamental core beliefs could be safely held.

SOCRATES

True that is. When the ideas and practices of the enlightened sages are introduced into a prophetic culture, it is likely to create conflicts as well as attempts to create a synthesis with them.

JESUS

In that conclusion, you brought together so many things I have thought and experienced that I would really like to see in more detail, or better yet by example.

SOCRATES

Rather than my explaining my conclusion, why not review how this conflict and these attempts at the synthesis took place in Judaism?

JESUS

Even though Judaism is many things and takes on many forms, the core beliefs do not change. In every prophetic religious tradition, not only Judaism, there are many voices urging that this and that needs to be done, but core beliefs retain their grip on the soul. There are times when core beliefs can be reflected on, and to some degree modified under the force of the new, but when a crisis comes, there is always the force to reestablish the old.

SOCRATES

Pleased I am to reflect upon that force and more so to learn how it relates to the new. What form do you see it has taken?

JESUS

It is true that we have a prophetic tradition, but we, too, have our sages. We call the sage movement the role of the priest, or the rabbi. It is a profound movement from prophet to sage. When you and I say that there is no place where God is not, then we are saying the old notion of a God in Heaven has given way to the realization that the light of God reaches into everyone and all things while still being what it always is. This teaching is for the most part from our own sages. Under the guidance of the tales of the rabbi, each person sees what is to be seen which was never hidden. There is no truth that can remain hidden. It is like clouds obscuring the sun's rays that are swept away with the new light of dawn. Nothing is remote from the divine. I see you like that, Socrates. We should visit such teachings. The fusion of the Chasidic and Sephardic with the *Kabbalah* moves in this creatively profound way. The teachings of the Baal Shem Tov are most interesting to me. The *Openings of Wisdom* of Lussatto added the insight into the "ten Sefirot" of the mental powers found in the "ten Sefirot" of the *Kabbalah*.

SOCRATES

Well said. I am very pleased to hear of it. It is likely to be similar to what can be seen in Plato's *Parmenides*. There you can find the nine hypotheses, and with Zeno's, you have the ten. Each system deals with the powers of the mind. It can be seen that the Wisdom traditions cut across all traditions. From what I have heard, Plato's *Parmenides* has brought forth the *Kabbalah* in the Sephardic tradition and it has been glowing ever since. After our talk, I, too, plan to make a few heavenly visits with those you mention who are exploring these things.

JESUS

I should not let your praise obscure the point you are making. From what you have attested to, we need to say something about this entrance of the *Kabbalah* into tradition. I cannot hesitate to say a truth even if some might prefer it otherwise. Indeed, if the source of the *Kabbalah* is the *Parmenides*, then that means they fit in the class of interpreters that are akin to our fourth class since they use the new to patch up the old.

CHORUS

Here we are again. Making divisions and classes and sticking members into them is the mark of analysis. Neither of them had the courage to speak out and admit that the only reason they didn't write anything down was because they probably couldn't put it into words. No one grasped what either of them was doing anyway. Their teachings offered everything to those in Heaven and delivered nothing on Earth. Clearly, they both had faults because they took on a body. Did they fail in their so-called mission? Who among their followers ever really understood a single thing they said? Logic and understanding go just so far and the rest of the way goes with faith and belief. All this talk of making distinctions or divisions within classes is a diversion. Just notice how the appeal to Truth has a ring of something noble and good. Let's not forget: They didn't express this so-called truth, did they? I didn't hear anything about love, only logic. Everyone can only take in what fits into their past, and all the rest is left on the plate to be thrown out. That's what. Now, look at this absurdity. Calling on Plato's *Parmenides*. That is a stupid logical work of no importance. What fool would believe the influence of Parmenides could possibly create a spiritual work such as the *Kabbalah?* Go ahead and add it to a movement that thinks the void is filled with God. Where will this nonsense end?

Anti-chorus

Shouts again from the fools out there. Wake up! Your bitterness clouds your words. Are you sharing how you feel about these two sages, or are you describing some flaw in what they have said or done? We heard it and hope you did too. Take seriously that someone right here is going to offer the only way Truth can become present and visible to us all. Can you suspend your bitterness and let what follows develop naturally through this dialogue? So, sit down and listen.

Socrates

Before we go further with our divisions, it may be important to ask if we, unknowingly, contributed to the problem. Could it possibly be that part of the problem is ours? Since neither of us left any writings, the task of presenting our work was left for others. Is the burden of that task too much for those who cannot endure the profound nature of that light? The more immediate writings that followed my death were Plato, then Aristotle and Gorgias. Later, there were others, and each has their strengths and weaknesses. You, of course, had your share of those who interpreted your mission.

JESUS

Very true, Socrates, and after my death there were many interpreters who wrote out their gospels and nearly all but four went up in flames. As you know, some that were hidden escaped destruction and have been unearthed in Egypt. Among my interpreters, many simply ignored what I said and did. Then there are those who substituted their own beliefs and expressed them as if they were mine.

SOCRATES

It looks like we identified our third division; because those who substitute beliefs to block the emergence of the true and original we can call the deniers and falsifiers who function as wolves in sheep's clothing.

JESUS

Yes, among them were the followers of Paul. His followers put the torch to whatever offered a picture different than that of their own making. Curiously, Paul was the one they believed, even though he stoned to death my earliest followers and chose not to include any of my work in his letters. Surely, Socrates, that was the same for you and for some of your interpreters. However, he did include one statement of my ministry, but it is not in the gospels.

SOCRATES

Yes, Jesus, that is a common feature among those who would be our interpreters. You had your Paul and I had Aristotle, and that difference doesn't make much difference. Your Paul and my Aristotle both believed they alone understood our teachings. Without touching what was there to be seen, they crafted what they wanted to see. Yes, I also had Plato and Gorgias; the former saw much, and the latter saw little. Truly, shall we say that it is inevitable that we cannot be truly understood unless those seeking Truth share in the same divine enlightening vision that we shared, and then go and function as we did?

JESUS

As it is said, those who only follow the literal word are not able to grasp the meaning of the Word, Socrates. The unfolding of the Word is like a garden of the Logos and each seed brings forth its unique flowering. The beauty of the garden reflects the order and structure without which nothing can bloom with the majesty and power of the Logos. He who lacks the vision of the Logos is like a man seeking to know himself by studying his footprints in the sand.

SOCRATES

Difficult it may be; however, would you say that Paul denied what you proclaimed? I ask that because it would be helpful if you first stated the principal ideas of Paul's doctrine. After that, we can then focus on his differences from your own work.

JESUS

I do say we are proceeding rightly to first make clear what his message is. He made the claim that I was the only Son of God, a truly pre-existing divine being. I was said to have died on the cross, and in doing so, made atonement for the sins of mankind. My resurrection, he said, marks the beginning of a cosmic catastrophe, ending with the saved believers ascended into Heaven and all the rest of life destroyed. Death, he says, is abolished, and the demonic forces lose their power. My resurrection is said to place me at the right hand of God, making me lord and king. Further, he says, I will return on the clouds of Heaven to redeem the saved and bring the final judgment of man. From this time on, there will be no more suffering, sin, or death. Paul believed he would be present to experience this final end. He announces that those who join his church and follow the rituals of baptism and partake of the Eucharist will gain salvation after the resurrection. The saved become sons of God and gain eternal life with me in the Heavens. His was a carefully crafted message. It is repeated endlessly, and it lulls to sleep the souls of his followers, who can then forget what is said by others and by me.

SOCRATES

And you say that none of these sayings came from your own teachings? Did he not say that he was an apostle by God's will? From what I have heard, he said he was commissioned by the will of God; that is no small claim. But does that not mean he places himself, at least, as an equal with you, or surpasses you? Did Paul warn his followers to beware of any of the sayings of the other future gospels? Did that not apply to those of the New Testament?

JESUS

Yes, he not only warned them about the other gospels, but also called himself my apostle at God's call. Yet his teachings do not report anything of my earthly ministry, and he freely added what I never said.

SOCRATES

I appreciate the depth of your vision of Paul. It does raise a difficulty for me. He built a system of churches and departed from your own teachings. Did not those who followed Paul realize he distorted your own teachings? Did they not ignore Peter's role and adopt Paul?

JESUS

Socrates, you have always had this reputation of jumping directly into the heart of every issue, and here it is again. If my goal was not to establish a church but to provide a way to the Kingdom of God, then what interest would I have had in building an empire of churches? That was Paul's doing. You know Paul ignored my earthly ministry and chose to center his church entirely upon the significance of his idea of my presumed resurrection. His church added those ideas to my ministry after my death. Among the gospel writers, the earliest, Mark, lacks a resurrection account. The church added it to his gospel many centuries later. The other gospel writers drew heavily upon Mark and also added material from even earlier sources than those Mark used. Both Matthew and Luke drew from material that Mark ignored, and since they do not stress the esotericism of Mark, theirs is a public doctrine. Is it not curious that what Paul put in his account is not in Mark, and what Mark said, Paul ignores completely? Sure enough, the last gospel writer, John, was aware of this drama and sought to save Paul's doctrine by combining both into his account.

SOCRATES

I find that curious because from what I heard, Paul didn't have a major conversion experience on the road to Damascus.

JESUS

Luke added several very important parts to Paul's account of his conversion experience that he never said of himself.

SOCRATES

What's that? Did Luke repeat the same account, or did they differ? If they differ widely, why did he create their differences?

JESUS

Now that is not an easy question to answer because altogether there are four accounts of that experience, and none agree with the others. The most divergent of them is Paul's, and his conversion experience is the most modest of the descriptions.

SOCRATES

Perhaps it is the same old story. Some followers always add what had no part in their masters' teachings. It is nothing new; it is the same sad story. When beliefs go beyond what believers can believe, they add to our doctrines their own beliefs. Let me put that aside and ask, was not the Jesus of Mark's Gospel considered to be the embodiment of divine Wisdom?

JESUS

Well, you are asking if Mark's Jesus was beyond all others in Wisdom. When the scribe asked which of the commandments is first, the answer of Mark's Jesus combined the first and the second. He answered that God is not only one but that there is no other than he. Then he went on to say that you should love your God with all your heart, soul, mind, and strength. The scribe added, "and with all your understanding." As for the second commandment about loving one's neighbor as oneself, the scribe added, "that is greater than all the burnt offerings and sacrifices." When Mark's Jesus heard these additions, he said that the scribe, "having mind, was not far from the Kingdom of God." None of the other gospels report the superiority of the scribe's comments, nor that judgment, only Mark.

SOCRATES

Yes, Mark's Jesus acknowledged the scribe's superior answer and dignified it with his claim that it meant the scribe was not far from the Kingdom of God. So, Mind plays a major role in that statement.

JESUS

Actually, in that report the scribe noticed that I left out the role of understanding in the love of God, and that was an important omission.

Socrates

Yes, you were being corrected. It is important within my philosophy because the idea of understanding is seeing a kinship between the *Logos* and *Nous*, or the *Logos* and the Intellect.

Jesus

I find that as interesting as you do. Did you know that Mark often cites the need to understand, rather than believe?

Socrates

I will enjoy looking at that later. As for now, would you say that linking these two commandments with the theme of love is Mark's vision of the role of love in your teachings? Did Paul offer the same view of love as Mark?

Jesus

Another good question there, Socrates. Paul argues that God showed his love by giving his only son to humanity so that they may be saved. He offers that I died for man's sins. Then Paul adds in several places that the second commandment, to "love thy neighbor," is an act of charity. You, of course, would see the core beliefs in evidence here. Mark, as you may know, never said that I was God's only son. But, yes, this theme is picked up in the other gospels and, especially, in the Gospel of John.

Socrates

Does dying for man's sins wipe out sin? What does it mean to say that you die for their sins? Does that mean one can go out and commit again—the sins that had been forgiven? Is there no learning why one committed those sins? How is someone benefited if their sins are forgiven, if they have not understood why they committed those sins in the first place?

JESUS

The guilt is lifted from one's shoulders, the anxiety of having betrayed your God is absolved, and you can settle back and start again.

SOCRATES

We are surfacing another problem with Paul. I will assume that it does work. I am not disputing that; I am only asking if the individual has learned anything as to the origin of their misdeed. The question turns on whether it is wise to lift what needs to be known from those who most need to know. Let me put the issue in another way. How wise are you shown to be? How wise is the God Mark portrays him to be? Are there any references that show that Mark's Jesus is all knowing and wise, or are there other episodes that challenge that image?

JESUS

Yes, another example is needed to show this point. We can see that in Mark's Jesus when he had to recognize the superior stance of a Greek woman. She had pleaded with him to cast a demon out of her daughter. He answered that it was not fair to throw to dogs the children's bread of his teachings. She answered that even dogs can feed on the crumbs that fall from the table. He saw the profundity of her answer, the shallowness of his own, and did as she desired.

SOCRATES

Surely, that does make your point and does it twice. I would like to return to that theme of love, for the role of love among those in my tradition has a wider, an essential, and vital force in the way of the philosopher.

JESUS

Then it is your turn to share this wider vision of love. I have set out some points from my followers. Would you do the same from yours?

Socrates

Yes, but first I should say that we need to be careful when describing love to distinguish the roles and meaning of love as it functions with the lover, with the beloved, and in the act of loving. Behind these distinctions is the creativity of love in bringing to birth what is the consequence of that loving. In our philosophy, there is an intimate connection between the Logos and love, or the role of reason and love. It is for this reason that these two ideas are linked to the idea of midwifery in our philosophy.

If we begin with the mystery of love, we need to see that Plato starts his exploration into the nature of the origin of love in the Cosmos. He then explores the power of love through a model of love's domain as a mean between the immortal and the mortal, or between wisdom and ignorance, and, finally, between gods and man. To open up the dynamics of love, he introduces his myth of Poverty, Plenty, Love, and Aphrodite, thereby linking love as a medium between God and mankind. In doing this, he shows just how each of the levels of love matches the cognitive functions of ignorance, right opinion, understanding, and knowledge, or Wisdom. These ways of relating to knowing express the way the Logos unfolds as love becomes more comprehensive and extensive.

Jesus

Well, there you go again. You add so much in a few words. I am intrigued by what you are saying and would like to hear more about these ideas. However, I do have a lingering question. You put ignorance into the class of cognition, but isn't ignorance the total lack of any kind of knowing, or cognition?

Socrates

There are different kinds of ignorance. Here it means the state of mind of those who believe they know and boldly answer what they think they know, but then they are brought to see that they are wrong and have to admit they know nothing about what they thought they knew. In that state, they are as puzzled as puzzled can be. It has been called being stung as if by a stingray.

JESUS

That is good; now would you explore further how your Plato brings Love and Logos into a unity?

SOCRATES

Gladly, for it gives me pleasure to recall such ideas. The idea of love inspires those seeking fame and renown, those seeking the pleasures of lovemaking and bringing to birth children, those craftsmen, artists, and poets, and those seeking to bring justice within their families and cities. The highest among them are those seeking Justice and Wisdom since they are driven by a love to participate in the realm of the sacred. Should you be interested in reflecting on how Plato brings us to the highest expression of Love in the quest for Wisdom, we should turn to his *Symposium* and *Phaedrus*.

JESUS

Well, Socrates, I am waiting to hear more.

SOCRATES

In his *Symposium*, he starts with Love expressing itself in the love of beautiful bodies and in beautiful logos, or speeches. Then he adds that it is necessary to see that the beauty in all bodies is the same, and to go on to love those who have beautiful souls, and then to beget beautiful logos so the young can find in love something noble and good. He moves on to urge the love of beauty in our cities and customs, so that one can see a wider scope for love in the quest for Beauty. These early stages lead to seeing beauty in different kinds of knowledge. Surely we know that this kind of knowledge shines forth from the very source of Love and the *Logos*. For it is this that prepares the soul for the final vision of Beauty itself. The experience of Beauty opens the mind to the profound, for it alone can experience it. The experience is described with carefully chosen superlatives and balanced by negatives. The experience of Beauty unfolds the nature of Reality as Truth. It is from this state that a true excellence can emerge; it is the crowning experience of the philosopher, brought into being by love and perfected by the *Logos*.

Jesus

Is there more I should hear that describes the teacher and student relationship than these steps or stages?

Socrates

If the teacher finds a soul that is open, generous, and dedicated to the pursuit of philosophy, Plato says that he welcomes the two together, body and soul, and cultivates the relationship through talks about excellence and shares with his student what a good man ought to be and do. As a result of what they share, the student gives birth to what can be said to rival Homer and Hesiod.

Jesus

Now, Socrates, are you saying that Plato realized that his work would continue and rival the divinely inspired works of Homer and Hesiod? Surely, that is granting it a very high honor.

Socrates

You are right to ask that, and the answer is that Plato says it ranks higher than even those who established the first rational laws and even beyond the works of both Hellenes and barbarians.

JESUS

I wonder if I should say, "Good heavens, Socrates, what a splendid vision you describe." Awakening this profound idea of understanding is to prepare one for the Noetic vision of Reality. Now, can there be more to that from the other work, the one you called *Phaedrus?*

SOCRATES

Yes, the way the lover should approach true Beauty and join her in a sacred union is given an artful form in this dialogue. The idea is simple enough. He presents it in terms that make it vivid and vital. If the desire for the beloved is joined with the need to preserve and cultivate a meaningful relationship, then the manner of the courtship must be gentle, sincere, and include an understanding of the beloved. The opposite way ruins it. The difficulty in achieving this goal is that the soul of man combines nobility and fairness with powerful emotional drives that want instant gratification. With the struggle between these two forces, reason is forced to control the one desire and subdue the other. If it is successful in this struggle, it gains the beloved, and if not, it faces failure and shame.

The image he presents of this struggle is the charioteer trying to manage the conflicting desires of his two powerful horses. The plot of the drama focuses on the struggle for spiritual enlightenment; this always occurs because there is no beloved more beautiful or more real than that experience of true enlightenment. If the approach to the beloved is as a rash lover, all is lost. The difference between the struggle of those seeking earthly beauty and those seeking the magnificent divine Beauty is as vast as can be imagined. As Plato puts it, if the human eyes could be brought to see and behold divine Beauty, a terrible love would be aroused that would be uncontrollable. Thus, the way to the divine is the way the very passionate lover must learn to cultivate and gain the beloved. Truly it is a very beautifully told story that is as profound as it is true.

JESUS

I see that there is a depth behind these remarks of yours. This idea of Love gives me much to reflect upon. You grasp the very dynamics of loving beautifully. So, in loving one's beloved, one learns the way to the divine. The differences between the mortal and the immortal are the extremes that you reconcile in the mean. In learning the nature of the meaning of differences, it creates the condition for a higher union. Could you say more about this theme, Socrates?

SOCRATES

Yes, the mystery of Love is not in loving sameness, for it is in learning the meaning of difference that a true loving is achieved.

JESUS

Yes, that is true. Here you present the mystery of the extremes, and with them I suspect you will find the meaning of the mean. I see you are saying the same thing for the extremes as you would for poverty and wealth, or poverty and progress.

SOCRATES

Yes, and the idea of finding the harmony in a world of extremes is the very goal in our Intelligible Cosmos.

JESUS

There can be little doubt that Plato's idea of Love and the *Logos* far excels that of Paul and his followers.

SOCRATES

So, it is a certainty that we shall say that Paul is as ignorant of the loftiness of your teachings as he is of your philosophy. He substitutes his own limited theology for yours; then he is a denier of what you put forward. From what you have said, it looks like Mark may be our newcomer, the fifth division, since he denies what the denier proclaims. Curious it is, and interesting.

Jesus

Well, I agree that it does make him a member of a new division, the fifth.

Socrates

True it is, and we can call Mark the slayer of the falsifier and denier, Paul.

Chorus

What just happened? This is absurd. Against revealed truth, a mere argument has no weight. Those who believe can't be shaken by this logic-chopping argument. Collective belief has power, and this little argument has no effect on the enormity of what Paul declared. Paul declared that the utmost significance of Jesus' resurrection is what Christianity is all about. Paul merely toasted it to the heavens and gave us a way to free our souls of suffering in sin. The past suffering over one's sins is past. A sinner is forgiven of his trespasses by being justified by his faith. And you no longer have to suffer guilt since you have been justified by your faith as well. So that phony argument you just heard has no force; it is like trying to topple Mount Everest with the push of your hand. What you do here is a crazy myth wrapped around an absurdity. You can't love God as you would a woman. No, they have to be kept in their place and conform to the law. You don't have to believe, but look at what you get for believing. No one ever taught you to believe. Take a look. Sure thing, they don't have to believe it, but you have to know one thing. Listen to this for a truth: whatever a believer believes is true to them to whom it seems so. Who can say something is not believable to him to whom it seems so? Who can say what is sin and suffering? You can only experience it and that's all. Another absurdity is looking for faults in Mark's Gospel, because you either accept Jesus' account of his miracles or you are left out and can't believe in the miraculous, and that means you are dead to faith.

Anti-Chorus

Are you afraid to ask if this argument is true? Who else has seen it? Do you allow yourself to wonder just what effects this kind of reasoning has on the systems that have claimed otherwise? Are you worried what other arguments are yet to come? State what is said, that the model of the dialectic is in force. Does going this way shake what you have taken as true? Go ahead and say it. Does believing make it true? Why not leave now before you hear more? How come you are staying to hear more? Is your anger burning more furiously when you hear what you can't believe?

Socrates

Could you fill me in on the background of your exploration because all I have heard is that Mark has been said to be the earliest, followed by Matthew, Luke, and John?

Jesus

Sure thing. You see that Mark supplies the narrative structure for those other gospel writers. It is obvious that both Matthew and Luke copied heavily from Mark, but John covers several points that are found in Paul's doctrine. What is interesting is that you can't find Paul in Mark. Rather, Mark rejects each claim put forward by Paul and also adds a rejection of the tradition of Moses and Elijah.

Socrates

Interesting that what was not a part became a part. Now, as you did with Paul, are you going to do the same with Mark?

JESUS

Let me use your mode of reasoning and put forth what is there to be seen. To do that let us first look at the inherent problems that Mark outlines in his Gospel. You see, Socrates, he describes my journey so beautifully that unless one sees the points he is making, it is entirely possible to be caught up in the beauty and ignore his meaning. Doing so will make it much easier to see Paul's view of God and man's relation to God as something that is simply ignored in Mark.

SOCRATES

Interesting way you have of going; a two-level exploration will bring the house down.

JESUS

So, right from the beginning, Mark shows I am not following the path of John the Baptist since I am not going around baptizing for the forgiveness of sins. Then there is the problem of the consequences of a sage or teacher choosing his disciples, or his students, since the success or failure of those taught depends on the ability of a teacher to communicate his teaching, and for the students to have the commitment and aptitude to learn what is set before them to master. Clearly, Mark portrays me as a failure on two counts. He shows that my inner circle of disciples fails to grasp my parables. Even after they are given the key to the fundamental sower parable, they are still unable to apply it to the other parables. If these keys to entering the Kingdom of God were available to all, there would be no need for this esoteric understanding of the parables, nor the need for an inner circle. Yet, the understanding of these parables is said to be the only way to gain access to the Kingdom of God. Mark has my followers turn away from me at my hour of crisis. It raises a curious question: Could all the disciples, or even a few, have entered that Kingdom of God state of mind and yet turn away and flee?

However, it is not just the parables that are pointed to as the essential objects to understanding. Mark has me teaching in the temples without saying what I taught. His account of my miracles builds and reaches the high point with the feeding of the 4,000 and 5,000, but none of those cured or the miracle witnesses are admitted to my inner circle. Mark has me insisting that my inner circle understand not only the nature of the feedings, but also the meaning of the leftovers, the debris. What was ignored and swept away now has meaning, and it is of the utmost for my followers to fathom.

Socrates

You have made an important point here. I would like you to express once more their failure to understand.

Jesus

Yes, it is important and much follows from it. Let me say that in their failure to understand they are urged to beware of the leaven of the Herodians and Pharisees. The warning came after that feeding when the disciples asked for bread, knowing there wasn't any among them. Again, what is ignored and swept away now has a meaning. For they were asked if they knew the meaning of the amount of the food that was left over from the two feedings. Thus it is of the utmost importance for his followers to realize that the least little thing that Jesus does has meaning to be fathomed, since to be in awe of the miraculous is one thing, but to understand the significance of both feedings in terms of their consequences leads, he says, to the Kingdom of God.

Socrates

Yes, it is good to hear that from you.

Jesus

Mark showed that even though the disciples were warned to beware of the leaven of the Pharisees and the Herodians they were unable to perceive how that warning related to the feeding miracles and to their own actions.

Socrates

If the state of mind that is necessary to enter that kingdom rests upon understanding the meaning of those parables, then why do they need Jesus as a savior? Maybe I should ask where he got that role.

Jesus

So the savior role is the next target. In Mark, we learn that after Jesus selects Peter, James, and John to accompany him to the mountain top, he then describes the mystical experience of divine luminosity and out of it appears Moses and Elijah. They are said to have dialogued with Jesus. We learn nothing about that dialogue, nor do we learn why the disciples were told not to tell anyone about what they had seen until after I arose from the dead. They asked if they could build three tabernacles on that spot, one for Moses, one for Elijah, and one for me. Is it not strange that none of the churches celebrate the transfiguration by building such tabernacles in their churches?

The actions that followed this personification brought about a dismal failure. The drama shifts to acting out the predicted passion story. Accepting the title of being the Son of David is claiming the title of a king of Israel, which meant usurping the rule of Pontius Pilate. Arrest, trial, punishment, and death justly follow for anyone acting out that claim. It is treason. The failure played itself out in that last plaintive cry on the cross, "My God, my God, why hast thou forsaken me?" Mark has me announcing that God forsook me since he didn't care to save me on the cross.

The opening of his Gospel has the voice of Heaven announcing, "Here is my beloved Son" and ends with those last words of Jesus. Clearly, that means either God abandons his son or that he wasn't the Son of God. What is this story? A failed sage with a fine noble cause, but he gave up his sage-like function after his illumination.

After identifying with his ancient prophets, he entered the political world, claiming for himself the role of a king, the Son of David under his God's care and vision. Pontius Pilate saw through the absurdity of this claim. This role he assumed turned into disillusionment when he had to face his failed vision.

Socrates

So, as readers of Mark, we experience the tale of a noble man whose fate was of his own making, which was taking on a mission beyond the possible.

Perhaps later we could find the opportunity to discuss that dialogue you are said to have had with Moses and Elijah. Is it not true that after any major experience, including that transfiguration, we dwell upon it and draw conclusions from it? Surely, the more profound the experience, the more likely we are to draw conclusions about it. In my philosophy we draw from Parmenides this principle, because after he experienced the revelation from the Goddess, he framed his understanding of its meaning and called it his hypothesis. I would like to hear from you what you concluded, since much followed and changed after your own transfiguration experience, did it not?

Jesus

Yes, and that's very likely to be of interest. But you are linking Mark's account of me to a Greek tragedy and right now I find that more important to discuss. I would like to hear you unfold what you see in that. As I recall, the idea of a tragedy must have a hero who is brought to the realization that he created his own suffering.

I believe the principle is that in ignoring what should have been known one creates one's own fatal drama, or destiny. I don't see how that fits Mark's account.

SOCRATES

In considering the elements of a tragedy, Mark is not a tragic tale, but is instead a pathetic tale. It could have been avoided. Those who attend the tragedies know what a tragedy is. The tragic hero ignored things of his past he should have attended to and dealt with. Man forgets what he should remember and remembers the trivia he should forget. His ignorance crowned his folly with pathos. Pity is what the audience has for the hero, and they fear that they might share in the hero's fate. We are shaken by his ignorance and can only stand in horror at what could easily have been avoided.

The character of the hero contains the drama of the play. The plot spins out the hero's actions. The drama of the tragedy has a reversal of fortune. It reveals past forgotten or unsuspected acts of violence, but the consequences play out their drama with deadly accuracy. The final self-inflicted violence upon the hero is played out before the audience. It is known to all that had the fundamental error in judgment been avoided, there would have been no tragedy.

JESUS

Yes, it is a victory for a culture to create and then keep uppermost in their mind these tragedies. Do these tragedies have a structure to them? I ask that because I wonder if Mark's drama was borrowed from these tragedies.

SOCRATES

Good question you have there. There are those who find six natural divisions that are present in tragedies. Aristotle has the divisions, and they are well worked out. See if Mark's Gospel can fit into that model. The difference that I see is that at the ending of a tragedy the hero awakens to his folly, but not so in the gospels, since you end in a forlorn, abandoned, and needlessly suffering role.

JESUS

Now, I also will take the time later to delve further into that very idea. It shows a masterful grasp of principles, and if Mark used them to craft his work, that would be crafting the drama artfully. It does serve to create a new religious image for man. It had been understood to be the death of the hero. It ushered in a new role for the sage as one abandoned by the divine. His ignominious death is interpreted by Paul to be God's sacrifice for man's sins. However, I must say that it depends upon several points you have surfaced.

SOCRATES

So a failure turns into a victory. If you take that as the death of the hero, it ends the sage as the ideal. A new image, a new ideal, is being put forward. However, I will always wonder what it means to sacrifice for man's mistakes, faults, errors, and maybe even for his sins. For my own philosophy, it is only possible to grow if one has the courage to discover why one has faulted or been wrong. It is an opportunity to discover why the error was made. The act itself must have begun in believing one was justified in what one was doing.

Taking that step of interpreting the death as the ideal of sacrifice and as a model for understanding renders the understanding of the event into something impotent, since a saving God doesn't save his son.

JESUS

I enjoyed the way you brought all these ideas together. I grasp the particular and you supply the general. Wonderful it is.

SOCRATES

The last piece to look at is that idea of the Son of God. Affirming or denying this claim has had many consequences, has it not? Is it not an important issue to review with care?

JESUS

You are correct in that. Consider that the rejection of the title, "the only Son of God," which was assigned by Paul, and later by John's Gospel, is highlighted and reversed in Mark. To make his point, Mark has a Roman gladiator at the crucifixion scene viewing my death on the cross; he says to all that there is 'a' Son of God, not 'the' Son of God. Surely, as it is known, the church translators switched the term 'a' to 'the,' making it into the singular and signifying the one and only son. Nowhere else in his Gospel is that title accepted by Mark.

SOCRATES

Good call there, Jesus, and how did Mark conclude this masterful rejection of Paul?

JESUS

The crowning rejection of Paul lies in the ending of Mark's Gospel. The last scene is at the opening of the empty tomb. Yes, the youth did say that he had arisen, but is that evidence that he entered heaven? He left it at that, no evidence of resurrection, and no post resurrection appearances before his inner circle. The last twelve verses that include post resurrection appearances were added to his Gospel several hundred years after that Gospel was written. Mark's Gospel was the first and the other gospels that followed tried their best to modify and change what Mark had done, but it is still there to be seen. To avoid what is obvious, the church taught Paul and supported this fabrication with quotes from the other gospels. For if they couldn't save Paul, there would be no church for believers.

SOCRATES

Truly a fine analysis, Jesus, your adaptation has the depth and integrity that naturally springs from you. As Mark would have it, your actions follow the "book," the scriptures, while I follow my divine voice. My way was risking in action what was framed both by my practice and my meditation and tempered by my inner voice, while yours was well-known and carefully set out in steps and stages.

JESUS

After our journey, we are concluding that Paul's theology began as a new form of the core beliefs of Judaism, and whether or not we agree with it, we can say that it is a way of understanding ultimate concerns. So, while it is not your kind of philosophy, it is a philosophy for the many.

SOCRATES

Yes, we have understood his theology, and since it is a view of the nature of God, it is a theology, but it is not a philosophical way of understanding.

JESUS

What's that? It wasn't philosophical? Would you explain what you mean?

SOCRATES

The Abrahamic religions are a class of beliefs, and they should be understood as members of a class. Equally, we must also see the implications of what follows if there were no such religions.

JESUS

I think that what you say needs an explanation. It raises an old question for me. Why do you have to discuss the question in terms of negatives? If the color green exists, then what advantage do you find in going through all the effort to discuss the negative case, if green is not? If something is, why do you have to explain what follows if it is not?

SOCRATES

Consider this question. What would you say if we could show that these Abrahamic religions have a particular effect upon their followers, but that there are other things that can produce those same effects? Certainly, then, these religions are not unique, since other things can duplicate what they do. Again, if that were true, then would there be any reason one would choose to belong to them if you can get the same thing without being a member of that religion?

JESUS

Now, that is curious. You wouldn't need to believe in God if you could get the same benefits by believing in something else. What a curious way of reasoning. However, I do see your point and I'd like to see that kind of reasoning with this idea.

SOCRATES

Then we will have to describe how we understand these religions as a class in which all their divisions can be shown to be merely members of the class. After my description of these religions, you will have to see if my description fits what is common and essential in each of them. If you agree that these Abrahamic religions fit into a common class, then we can show what must follow if they did not exist.

Jesus

Yes, I like that and if any new religion matches the general description, it would fit into that Abrahamic class, wouldn't it?

Socrates

Clearly, you caught my meaning. Now, let us proceed with our present task. The primary drive that attracts members to become believers in the Abrahamic religions is their need to believe that in becoming a particular part of a whole, that they will gain an identity, and that the whole that they subscribe to will offer protections and benefits. The participation in this whole offers members a chance to be a part of that whole much like the parts of a body fit into a body as a whole.

The chief gain will be a freedom from the severe sense of estrangement and guilt. They believe that only God could possibly forgive them of their sins since they fear he alone will punish them for the sins they have committed. They expect that through joining the religion, they will gain a freedom from this sense of estrangement and guilt. Then their sense of belonging expresses itself in joining with others in a kind of fellowship that gives the sense of being a vital part of a different kind of whole or a markedly different kind of community.

It is essentially joining in an idea that has a drama built around the notion of a final catastrophic end. In participating in this idea they give up alternate ways of thinking and acting so that they all experience the same state of being limited by participating only in that association, and other kinds of relationships are equally limited. This very sense of being limited extends to their relation to one another and to the whole. The whole has its demands, and they extend to each of its members, or parts. It is through this association that they all share a sense of unity with others.

However, in joining the association, there arises within them something different, which gives them a limitation in relation to one another and to the whole. For the whole is that which demands sacrifices. It stands above its members. The result is that they are alike one another in sharing the same relationship, but within themselves they are aware of being utterly opposed and unlike one another. The result is that each has the sense that they are separated from others and exist by themselves in spite of being members of the whole.

The mark that distinguishes each member is that they have the sense that they do not need any self-reflection and examination of themselves to discover the origin of their differences or the origin of their estrangement. Hence, they do not seek for meaning in themselves, or among themselves, or in the world around them.

Jesus

Now, how would you state the condition of the believers once they leave the system they had formerly committed themselves to?

Socrates

If those in this class of believers were to reject their idea of God, they would be left to themselves and be different than their former ways of being. The kinds of relating and their actions would not be available to them. They would now be other than each other in their group since they lost that sameness they had previously identified with. Without that sameness, they then would be other than each other. For, sharing this difference, they still possess what they formerly sought in that idea they had joined. Thus they become a mass of their differences. Without the beliefs that shaped their judgments and perceptions, all that would be left would be making decisions arbitrarily. They would appear to share in their differences, but behind that appearance of sharing would be an indiscriminate mass, since what formerly allowed them to make distinctions of a general kind would be absent.

Thus, without the conviction that general judgments are legitimate, they descend to the apparent safety of making only particular judgments. Their appearance of equality with one another would lack grounds, for if they found such conditions and grounds for belief, they would find something similar to what they left. Hence, they would appear to be similar in thinking and acting with others like themselves, but they would still see themselves as unlike themselves and each other. Their sense of separateness would diminish their sense of contact with one another since it lacked what formerly bound them together. The kind of reflection that would cause them to discover the root of their problems, or sins, is missing and when considered by them, it is rejected, because if they could purge themselves of their sins or problems, there would be no need for forgiveness and feeling justified by their faith in repeatedly being absolved of their sense of guilt by their participation in their faith.

Since their former belief had no place for self-reflection that leads to self-discovery, they continue to deny that power in themselves. We would say they lack what we call *ousia*, which is the intellectual power to know the Self and the nature of Reality.

Jesus

We are not strangers to the idea of the Self; indeed, as in John's Gospel, "All things came to be through the Self, and apart from the Self, not one thing came to be." You describe the predicament of believers very well. You must have studied them and have understood their nature. What kind of reflection brought you to see them in this way of yours?

Socrates

My deepest thanks for that. So, there is a kinship between our traditions. Later, I will acquaint myself with where else you use the idea of Self.

There is something in man that knows when he is asked to believe in something, that in accepting the belief, it changes him. Belief moves the soul in a certain way. It changes one's vision into its opposite, a limited vision. For all belief, when it is urged upon us, comes with another belief, and that is that it is true. There are different kinds of belief, but the kind we are talking about is believing something is true when there is not only nothing to support it, but it is in principle impossible for there to be anything to support it. The effect this has on the soul is that it experiences a limitation in its very being. Accepting the irrational as primary makes the use of the mind frivolous. Simply, the presence of being a self no longer is important since the irrational looms over all. The belief separates oneself from all else and it has a mode of existing that by itself suspends the rational desire to understand. Each believer intuitively knows all other believers in the same system experience this difference in their state of mind both within themselves and with others and that gives them a limitation. If ever they are free from the belief, they re-experience the freedom from the limitation of belief. Within themselves, they experience at the same time being limited by the belief, and they also know that without the belief they would experience a freedom or a sense of the limitless.

These two states have an effect on believers, for they are opposites of one another, and so within themselves and with others, they experience a sense of togetherness; and at the same time within themselves, they experience an opposition. Then, as we both know, such believing exists within oneself, but it does not give any mark of its presence, so believers borrow from their experience of sacrifice the proof that they believe; thus they keep alive a belief by drawing upon something that is alien, something that provides them with an assurance that they do believe. Therefore their mode of existence is that within themselves they are in conflict, and this persists as long as they are captured by the belief.

Jesus

From this, I can see why you say that those who walk away from the Abrahamic religions are not at all likely to seek other spiritual systems, unless those spiritual systems also lack the necessity for making general judgments. For while making such judgments is necessary in any metaphysical spiritual system, it is not so for the Abrahamic. I think I follow your reasoning about making negative judgments. It is very curious because it is necessary to think along the lines that you have expressed. You took the example of this class of thinking to the limit. You found relations that must follow like stepping stones along a shallow stream. May I assume, my dear Socrates, that this way of thinking is expressed more purely in your tradition?

SOCRATES

You're correct in that. You are a perceptive and profound thinker, my dear Jesus. This mode of thinking is the dialectic, and it was formulated by one of my teachers, Parmenides. If you would care to, you can see it in Plato's fine work called *Parmenides*. There you will see a work that sets out all the possible spiritual systems in strict metaphysical terms. It outlines four major systems and their denials, but above and beyond these you will find the very profound Hypothesis the One Self.

JESUS

I have had thoughts that are akin to what you have said, but which lack the precision. I will be sure to go over them after our talk.

SOCRATES

You are quite right, because the precision you will find there rests upon making and using a distinction most of mankind does not make. We call the highest and most accurate Idea of God the One. In using the Idea of One, you can link many ideas directly from that idea and this is what gains precision in our thought. Consider: the idea of oneness, whole, wholeness, perfect, complete, unity, and others are naturally linked to the Idea of the One. Those who traditionally use the idea of God instead of the One have a limited set of linking ideas. For in our philosophy these notions form a natural unity from which arguments about the supreme can more easily be made.

JESUS

Another good point you've made, Socrates. Is there something else you might say about those who depart from the Abrahamic religions?

SOCRATES

Yes, I could say that they are in a desperate state, but whether or not it is better than being in the denial is something worth discussing. The negative side of their departure is that they do not seek a more direct participation in the spiritual life through any philosophical-spiritual practice because it had never been a part of their thinking. Such believers seldom realize that what was forbidden and condemned has a lasting effect so that even in leaving these religious systems, they still maintain much of what was taught to them to fear. To be suspicious of speculation, to consider ideas other than those that are based and anchored in particulars, is considered by them to be foolish and sinful. Lacking completely in any participation in *ousia*, which is the profoundest mode of being, they gather within their common belief, that they do not understand, and this binds them together.

Thus when they leave, they retain these negative views, not realizing that these teachings were fundamental to their former beliefs.

CHORUS

Here's another stupid argument, nonsense piled on top of the absurd. These two make distinctions where there are no differences. Go ahead and show that there is no good reason to believe, and I'll laugh in your face. You just don't know what it is to be a believer, that's all. Paul gave us what can't be argued against. Why? Because there is no good reason to believe what you believe. If you need a reason to believe, you wouldn't be among true believers. That's why you need faith. It is not something to prove, so why pay attention to such arguments against Paul? You can always find a flaw in anything, so why trust reason? Belief is much stronger and more enduring than any idea held by some reason. So, your arguments are nothing other than your own resentment that you can't bring yourself to believe.

Anti-Chorus

You believe you can't go any further, so you are left with belief. You believe you are justified in quitting the search because you don't have the stomach to continue your search. All you want is a way to silence your own doubts and worries and return to the warm feeling of being childlike in your belief. You really want to silence those screaming voices you hear at night. So go ahead and pump yourself up with belief and watch what your belief rejects. Believers quit the quest for clarity and truth.

Jesus

I would like to ask, "What shall we say about Plato's understanding of your work?" However, before that, is it not even more important for you to set out not only what you call your philosophy, but also whatever practice is essential to this philosophy of yours. Then it will be easier to see Plato and Aristotle. How will we say that Plato gave a more comprehensive view of your work if we don't know your work? Did he include a spiritual dimension that neither Aristotle, nor Gorgias, nor Protagoras followed? How will we know if they included the important parts of your philosophy?

Socrates

Well, from what we have said, it seems likely that we will find that Plato tried to represent what I was doing, but must have left something out, and may have also added what I never said. As for Aristotle, that is easier, he just added his own beliefs as a substitute for what he couldn't accept from me. He is much like Paul, the denier, in that they both thought anything that came before them was incomplete and they believed that they alone saw what others failed to see.

JESUS

I do like the way we explored Paul and Mark. Let's begin the comparisons after you share just what the essential message of your philosophy is. For in doing that, it should help me see yours in comparison with Aristotle and Plato.

SOCRATES

Well, that is a thoughtful way to continue. Surely you do offer a perfect point of departure. It is first necessary for me to say that my philosophy is not something unique to me. In a real sense, I have no personal philosophy. I am one of those philosophers who stand in a long line, singing the same song about the Gods and their dealing with man. I may have gone further than some, just as some have said what I have said. Equally, in the future there will be others who will catch this most splendid of tunes of philosophy and join me in this song. So what have I come to? It is in this most fundamental analogy:

As that which is beyond all names and categories is the cause of that most brilliant light of Being, so too is this most brilliant light of Being to the Sun, or Helios.

Here is the most splendid of mean analogies. Its depth is marvelous to behold and understand. The analogy expresses that there is a parallel structure between Heaven and Earth, between the realm of the Mind and its transition to the Cosmos. The primary term is named the Good itself and second term, the divine luminosity, is also called the Idea of the Good. For when we stress this term,

Idea, we do so because in the Greek the word idea means to behold. To behold the Good is to behold it as the divine luminosity. The second ratio, or Logos, continues the creative power of creation from the metaphysical to the God, Helios, or from the divine luminosity to the Sun. To understand this analogy and to come to realize the depth of these two ratios is the task of my philosophy. The understanding that is shaped through this reflection brings the mind to recognize that the nature of Reality has an Intelligible permeating multileveled power that deserves the name, Logos. The understanding developed prepares the mind for visionary experience confirming for the philosopher that it is genuinely possible to be present before the Good itself.

As the sight of this Beauty of the divine luminosity awakens an intense desire for union with it, so too is the desire to participate in it most fully. The name we give to this desire is Love. For Love is the desire for the Beautiful and the Good. To experience it and understand it in depth is Wisdom, as the practice of being open to it and participating in it is an exalted kind of knowledge. Its goodness shines throughout and it becomes that to which one looks when forming an idea of what is just both in man and society.

JESUS

You speak truly, for the most brilliant light of Being is the Son of God; it is the manifestation of God, it is the presence of God, and as we enter into it we know that while we are what we have become, it stands majestically and profoundly itself as itself, or the self as the self. A true philosopher is a true mystic, and if the philosophy embraces as much as you have said, then it becomes the way of Wisdom.

SOCRATES

Yes, indeed, for I have left nothing undone that would keep me away from my goal. I often said that while there are many Thyrsus bearers, few there are who are true mystics. I made it clear that I am among those mystics, and I urge those about me to join in this practice.

As for some principle, I have urged those about me to pursue the second ratio of that analogy: the most luminous light of Being is to the sun, Helios. Why? Because the principle behind all suns in all galaxies cannot be a sun but the condition for suns to be. This principle is Helios, the condition for suns to be. The God Apollo is often connected to Helios and his temples are linked with the God Helios. Here is a divine becoming on two levels; the most primary terms are the God that transcends all description and the luminosity that needs all the superlatives in the attempt to match its splendor. These two ratios form the analogy, bringing a unity that reveals there is a parallel intelligible structure of our Cosmos. Understanding it and coming to know it is one of the goals of my philosophy. Once gained, this vision can become the standard for all that is called good, beautiful, and just. Here is the foundation of our search for fundamental principles and our psychology and ethics.

Jesus

Now, that was well said, Socrates. You link these ideas with your idea of Mind, do you not?

Socrates

Yes, indeed, after encountering that vision of the nature of Reality, I had urged those in my circle to take on the real task, which is to recognize that it is not different from Mind itself—not a mind, but Mind itself, seeing it as what is essentially our true Self and we call it Mind. It is true that we can call it Reality, or Wisdom, or Beauty itself, since these are different ways of expressing that majesty of that divine luminosity and these are called Ideas. The way to this state of Mind is open to all. This is why we have a rational approach to surfacing the very blocks to that experience.

Clearly, man is caught in his own beliefs and opinions that effectively block him from that vision. As those about me exhibit these false beliefs, I challenge them to defend their ideas. I question everyone I meet who lives with such false beliefs. I even question the most powerful in society and none can escape my quest to examine each and every one about how well they care for their soul. This, as you know, is my duty and role as a philosopher to my fellowman. God has assigned this duty to me, just as a commander would assign someone to a battlefield position. I should add that no better thing has happened to any city-state than my role as a gadfly to the state. As a citizen of this state, I fulfilled my role in every way. I obeyed the laws of this state because through the perfection of its laws, man becomes part of this Intelligible Cosmos. Be it as a soldier, or an official in that state, I did everything I could to show the excellence that guided my soul.

Jesus

You have said it well. I now understand much better the nature of your trial. You have awakened in me much that I knew without recognizing its depth.

Still, my dear Socrates, is it not true that these blocking beliefs spell out man's ignorance, yet are not known to them? You have to help them find what they never suspected was blocking them.

Socrates

Yes, what is not suspected remains unknown. Only questions can unearth the roots of ignorance, questions guided by the quest for Truth become dialogues. So I dialogue with those willing to enter into the search for Truth. Our dialogues are never confined to an inner circle. Those who care to sit in and listen to these dialogues see in another's problem aspects of their own.

Man only has a finite number of problems and each shares a basic motif with all others. Dreams are rich messages from the

Mind that can turn us about and keep us on the noblest journey, philosophy. The meaning of our dreams comes slowly to most, but it is all a matter of learning. Those who have gained insight into the language of dreams have learned to see a profound level of meaning in their relationships within themselves and with others. It is a rich source of learning of symbols, metaphors, and analogy, and in the ways of carrying on communications that brings us to the realization that we are all on a spiritual journey. This is the Logos emerging from within the rational pursuit of the Truth found in dreams. The common features of our spiritual struggle highlight their differences. For as Heaven is, so is Earth. It is through such analogies that I bring to birth a new kind of understanding.

In this philosophical search, we explore allegories and myths. The myths we reflect upon have parallels with the spiritual journey of man and can represent that journey with dramatic and philosophical charm. They both express and challenge seekers to unveil the drama cloaked in such images and symbols. The quest to resolve the meaning hidden in allegories is found in expanding analogies and finding parallel terms for each image and idea. Bringing these two together is the philosophical way for the cultivation of the understanding. With this inner development of one's understanding comes the very condition for gaining the vision of ultimate Reality.

Jesus

Your way of bringing understanding to Truth and enlightenment is very difficult for man to grasp, Socrates. The deep roots of ignorance remain untouched even after the most profound enlightenment experience.

Socrates

There are many who believe we are here to achieve enlightenment experiences, without realizing that there are many different stages of enlightenment. It is quite easy to believe, after a penetrating vision into the nature of Reality, that one is beyond good and bad. Being bathed in light easily conceals problems. Equally, one can appear free of problems without having been touched by the more profound spiritual experiences. Enlightenment gives insight into the nature of Reality. It does not give understanding of one's fundamental problems. Enlightenment experiences may lessen the power of one's problems without blocking or solving them. Problems can only be resolved by an understanding that answers the problem. We are here to solve our problems so that we can be free to pursue the Good itself.

Jesus

The role of understanding is essential to us both. I am reminded of Mark's repeated urging to understand. It is so important to the spiritual life and the quest for Wisdom. There are not many sages who delve as deeply as you and your followers have into the issue of ignorance. It certainly plays a major role in your own philosophy, doesn't it?

Socrates

True it is, Jesus. My philosophy is a Love of Wisdom, and it reaches a peak in the experience of that luminous light of Being. It brings the soul of the seeker to understand why that experience marks not the ultimate, but the penultimate point of their spiritual life. Yet, without that vision, there could never be that fundamental insight into the presence of Justice and Goodness at the core of Reality. I did try to make it clear to those who seek both understanding as well as that experience that our guiding analogy is simple enough. It all starts with light and ends with light. For as the divine luminosity brought forth the fiery Sun so, too, the Good itself reflected that divine luminosity of pure Being that has been called the Idea of the Good.

JESUS

As peaks are few, valleys are many, and as meadows are to grass and trees so they reflect a mystery to unearth. The heights are splendid, but most turn to confusion and bitterness as they face their human problems.

SOCRATES

Each person has reached his height; each height allows a vision whose scope is limited by its very height. The expression of that vision is the reach of the Mind. It is that which the mind of each has come to realize as his vision. Each person is an expression of the truths he has brought together into a unity. We live it and defend it. The willingness to share in an encounter with someone who is willing to share their most fundamental vision naturally challenges your own vision as it does theirs, at least to the extent that they are willing to participate with you in a review of their views. Surely, this is a challenge, for the review tests the understanding and truth of such views. The willingness to engage in dialogues that seek for the truth of one's vision turns upon itself and perfects it. This perfection is the perfection of the understanding towards the unfolding of a deeper Truth, and though Truth itself is elusive it is always worth the effort to draw her out. I test myself and anyone I meet who is willing to engage with me in the discovery of what it is we truly understand about ourselves and this reality we engage in. The ideas of life and death, the divine and human, wisdom, and ignorance, are the ideas I am drawn to and are perfected in exploring with others. Thus you see when I hear there are wise men and women in my area, I seek them out so that I can test again the clarity of my vision and the truthfulness of the ideas I have come to. You can say my talks are *Logos* meditations since they always weave within them the mystery of the Logos and how it unfolds its Truth in our every gesture, thought, perception, and act.

Jesus

And, Socrates, you are part of a tradition that has been crafted over hundreds of years, if not thousands, into a rational seeking culture. You Hellenes are rare among cultures. Here among the Abrahamics the struggle is different. We have a different origin; different myths guide our people. Surely we know that the many out there seek only to be entertained and not taught. You people have your great mysteries like the Panathenaea. For our part, we have a crying wall and a temple with law overriding everything. We don't seek to understand these things you regard as sacred nor do you ours. At best we can only stand in awe of what we dimly perceive yet recognize as wondrous. You reach for very profound principles in your talks, but that would fall on deaf ears here among the children of Abraham. The real question is what a teacher is, and is there a need for only one teacher for man's spiritual quest? With belief one does not have this issue, but who would dare say that belief can stand alone?

Socrates

Yes, it is very likely that the whole of man is involved in this quest and not merely a part. The problem with belief systems is that they do not stand alone. I mean that if one has a belief or has faith in something, then one needs an accompanying feeling or state of mind that attends it in order to feel secure in that belief. Sacrifice something you love, kill non-believers, go on crusades, struggle to convert someone else, feel something else and link that feeling to the belief and then you know you believe.

Understanding, knowing, and insight systems stand apart from such efforts to feel certainty over what has been reached. Understanding has its own state of mind and it is known for what it is. Those who seek to gain the certainty of knowing through understanding seek the state of knowledge in a transient arena that is incomplete and so they are always restless in their belief. However, true knowledge is that which is an unchanging permanent state.

Jesus

Yes, while knowledge culminates the spiritual quest, there are those who only caught a glimpse of its mystery yet pronounce loudly their fragment to the world. These are the ones who came to the mystery after some accident or traumatic event, or mushroom experience without the preparation of philosophy. Surely, as you know, there are some here who experience a glimpse of death and dying and share with others their newfound knowledge. I have a deep interest in learning what these people have experienced and what they have concluded about it, for they came to this experience without preparation or training.

Socrates

You are correct there, Jesus. Equally, I should add, Plato praises the need to understand dreams, and he stresses their importance. However, he does so without sharing insights into the way to reach the meaning of dreams. In the age I lived, people had a profound interest in dreams. The consequence of the failure to understand dreams was clear to these Hellenes. In Homer, we can see that Agamemnon's failure to understand the dream Zeus sent to him is a measure of that failure. Plato acknowledges that it is through dreams that one can gain knowledge of one's present and past, and insight into one's future. Once the spiritual door has been opened, many powers become available to one. Those who know about the Tibetan practice of *Thumo* can easily see the parallels in Plato's description of me as having the ability to withstand severe cold. He mentions my standing meditating in one spot for 24 hours as well as speaking of my prophetic powers. While he reports on these spiritual abilities and brings one to reflect on them, we do not find that Plato describes these practices from his own experience.

Jesus

It is clear there is a gap between teacher and student, and it may be that the student should wait until he has equaled his teacher before writing about his teacher's spiritual life. You may have shared such secrets, but for reasons Plato alone knows, he chose to keep them secret.

Socrates

Yes, that is true just as you say. Plato showed me confronting sophists and bringing them to task, but not unfolding these sacred mysteries of philosophy.

Jesus

Then could you say what else he ignored that was most central to your way of being and your philosophy?

Socrates

Yes, then I should add that Plato knew I often said that my companion in life was my inner spiritual voice, and that it kept me on the path of Wisdom. Plato did not share how man can cultivate his own sacred inner voice. Most men live with many different voices screaming one thing and another, much like those voices that bounce off the walls of a cave. Here again is that old saying that any master can help many without being able to make another a master like himself, just as masters of any art know far more than can be taught to another. Future sages will always find a way to add meaning to that inexhaustible mystery of our Being, and some may confront something unique to their age that needs to emerge because of the uniqueness of the age itself. Equally, there may be something unique about a master who is not capable of being imitated or taught.

JESUS

Yes, Socrates, I see the same as you. The urge among many Christian believers to imitate me is as noble as it is good. Since there are many interpreters, there are many models to imitate. How does one choose his model? Some choose wise and some foolish models, but there is likely to be none that can reproduce my own way of being.

SOCRATES

Those with many needs, Jesus, always choose the most vital for themselves without regard to what may be best for themselves or others. So, yes, in missing what is essential, they created a gap. Others that follow them call it a mystery. It is the same with my Plato. For where he mentions the two profoundly exalted states, The Good itself and the luminous light of Being, which is also called the Idea of the Good, he offers no insight into the passageway from the one to the other. He also describes the way to gain the vision of Beauty and then stresses the need to emerge from that state to seek that kind of human excellence that would make one immortal and a friend of the Gods. He stopped there, didn't he? Surely, sharing the meaning of these things could have benefited some. Did our commentators reach their own limits and so could say no more than they did?

JESUS

It leaves me to wonder if the fullest flowering of Plato's view of your own teaching and practice can bring to birth the kind of excellence that truly brings you to be a friend of the divine and immortal, if any man ever is. I know you put much into the study of dreams and visions, but in truth, I have learned this way is not without its dangers. Plato is incomplete, and that makes him an interpreter whose vision, while beautifully stated, was flawed and incomplete.

CHORUS

The roots of folly are now celebrated by a fool and preached to the blind. Gaining insights into Reality from dreams is not just absurd; it is totally and completely ludicrous. Belief in dreams makes fools of us all. Dreams are impossible to understand because they are leftover debris from our past. There is no ultimate anything. Ultimate cloaks, ultimate fictions, phooey is ultimate when it comes out of the mouths of philosophers. Don't talk about mind; there is no such thing. There is only a brain buzzing around impressions of things. Words without physical referent are empty sounds screaming in the wind.

ANTI-CHORUS

Instead of shouting meaningless phrases, why don't you see if you can learn what you believe is impossible? Listen to yourself and ask where your shouts come from. What propels your own nonsense? Fear of the mind drives your own absurdities. Quiet down and listen. Put your fear of being fooled aside. The fool fears his being a fool and that keeps him foolish.

JESUS

I find what you are saying is far from being obvious. Yet it has the ring of truth to it. However, the implications of all that you say are echoing through my mind. You are saying man's problems, all of them, are the effect of an induced ignorance that can be emptied of its duplicity. This ignorance, you are saying, can be directly studied and dispelled through exploratory dialogues on problems and dreams. So you have not only been busy confronting people who manifest their problems, but also drawing them into exploring their inner life of dreams. Most curious it is. I would like to hear more about how you understand the structure of dreams.

SOCRATES

Yes, the problems one acts out in one's life are the subjects of one's dreams. Behind every problem is a false belief of the Self and of the nature of our Reality. With the surfacing of the roots of these false beliefs, they fall away. The roots of the most vivacious problems or the minor irritations one ignores are always our having been deceived into believing something false. Ignorance is not a natural product of life. It is always the result of having been persuaded of something false. Ignorance is learned since its source is always in a false idea of the Self.

JESUS

How did these ideas come to you? They have the ring of truth about them. What sages from your past experience fashioned them with such penetrating skill?

SOCRATES

As my mother was a midwife who assisted women in the delivery of their child, so I am called a midwife because I assist men who are pregnant with unsuspected false ideas. Homer is our sage who taught us that even the worst among us can become as enlightened as it is possible to be. He showed us that as the roots of the pattern that dominated Achilles' ruinous wrath was learned from his surrogate mother, lord Phoenix, so Achilles was able to uncover this false way of being that he had learned and freed himself from its bonds to become the sage he became.

JESUS

From what I have heard, was it not through the Goddesses Athena and Thetis that Achilles was able to break through what had held him in the grip of his own folly?

SOCRATES

Achilles had to separate himself from both Goddesses and turn upon his own life, and through that self-examination he was able to free himself from his false beliefs about himself.

JESUS

You Hellenes fight fierce wars to defend these ideas that you have and so do the followers of Abraham, but your wars are fought for human concerns while those wars of the followers of Abraham follow the dictates of God.

SOCRATES

Yes, but the war against Troy was different since Homer tells us that the war was designed by Zeus so that we could learn about the nature of man. The lesson of that war was to show how the worst of men, Achilles, could turn about to become a godlike hero among us. It was through that learning that we have become superior to those ignorant of these teachings.

JESUS

Was your Achilles bathed in that divine luminosity that transfigures those who experience it? Did he reach the same state I had reached?

SOCRATES

Yes, Homer described him as he stood on the moat before his final battle with the Trojans, and the Goddess Athena opened him to that experience of a golden cloud wrapped around him that made his body blaze with a radiance that lit up the sky.

JESUS

Beautiful it must have been, and I can see that the divine has brought him to that divine oneness.

Now, then, my friend, Socrates, would you say then that Achilles overcame his sin that is common to all mankind?

SOCRATES

There is nothing that can coexist with that state other than itself. And there is no need to introduce the idea of sin, evil, or Satan to explain man's problems. To punish for believing something false never changes the belief. A God that punishes is no God at all. Man's true goal is to see that his problems spring from nothing else than having taken the appearance of truth of what appears so noble and true as if it is what is real and true. The appearance of virtue masks every act of vice.

JESUS

You state your beliefs with simplicity and power, and that I admire. If not sin, must there not be a counterforce that helps overcome this tragic dimension of everyday life? Your philosophy stresses the role of Mind turning reflectively upon itself to undercover false beliefs of the self as the primary force opposing the illusions and delusions of mankind. Could not that counterforce or negativity have an evil source rather than good?

SOCRATES

Your question goes to the heart of our difference. Would you not also include in your question the possibility that even though they may rid themselves of false beliefs of the self, they do not know if they have been deceived, and may still be subject to evil forces?

JESUS

Yes, that must be answered by you, must it not? We both know the divine luminosity, that divine transfiguration experience. I choose to follow the model of Abraham while you turned to philosophy, but which of us can say that one is better or higher than the other?

SOCRATES

Wisdom does not follow from that experience, or else we would both pursue the same cause.

JESUS

Socrates, I see here that we differ, for there can be nothing higher than that experience of the divine, for that experience is the presence of the very nature of God.

SOCRATES

Yes, it does raise a question, and I am pleased we can discuss it here. Let me put a few questions to you, Jesus. First, would you say that everything has a cause?

JESUS

Surely, as the sun rises each morning so too this can be said forever. Each thing is the effect of a cause and the cause springs from that higher cause, does not it, Socrates?

SOCRATES

And would you say even that experience of the Sun shining upon us has a cause? Or would not everything and every experience have a cause?

JESUS

Again, yes to that.

SOCRATES

Then that experience of divine luminosity, what we also call the most brilliant of Being, must also have a cause.

JESUS

Now, that is a strange conclusion, and even if it follows, there is still nothing higher than the experience.

SOCRATES

If a cause is always higher and has a greater status then its effect, then the cause of that luminosity must be greater and more profound. Again, is not the presence of God in that experience a manifestation of God and not the God itself?

JESUS

What have we here but a puzzle beyond all puzzles? If you call the highest the Self then I would say in that experience it is very clear that it can also be called the self or, as you philosophers call it, the One.

SOCRATES

Yes, that is true, it can be called the self; however, Jesus, would you not say that it too must have a cause if it is contained in an experience? And, would not what we have said apply to that as well? For, if all experience must have a cause, then is it not less than its cause? Did we not agree to that?

JESUS

Then, that experience of the self can only be called an image of the self, or a manifestation of the self. Now, that is more strange to me than anything else you have said, Socrates.

SOCRATES

Any image of the Self must always be less than itself, and the separation and difference between and image and that to which it is an image stands as appearance is to its reality since an image of the truth is false and an image of the divine is only an appearance and lacks the presence of itself.

JESUS

Much follows from what we have said, and caution must be our guide. For you are close to saying that the idea of God is less than the idea of the Self.

SOCRATES

The idea of God must always be separate and beyond any idea man can conceive of, but in being separate it is remote from Mankind, while the idea of self is not remote, but a necessary idea of one's existence. With God one needs belief, while there is no need for belief about whether or not one has a self. The issue is an old Hellenic one, and that is if you Know Thyself, do you know the self as the creator of all, the source of all, and nothing can be said of it that does not diminish its truth.

JESUS

Were you the author of this teaching about the Self?

SOCRATES

No, it is ancient. The idea of Know Thyself was celebrated at the temple of Apollo. My teacher, Parmenides, laid out his dialectical method to reach truth, and it was he who established a rational method of reasoning so that one can understand the Self and the Logos.

Jesus

So, we have seen that they are different from one another.

Socrates

Yes, and that difference shows itself as one being open to exploring the mind and the other not.

Jesus

From what you have said about Achilles breaking through his problems your people have a way to understand man's problems, and I think you believe your difference emerges from that kind of understanding. What I find curious is that you go on to attribute the same importance to the study of dreams, but I have not heard from you why or how you came to that strange conclusion. While all people dream, you study what the rest of us ignore. Let me make clear what it is that I believe. I mean no offense to you or your people, but most of us would think your reliance upon dreams as a way to understand oneself is far from the truth since unless they come from the divine are merely left-over fragments reappearing in dreams.

Socrates

What you ignore our people strive to understand because it is through the mind that we can know the mind. And, in coming to know the mind we grasp the need to say to one another that the self is the source of the mind's profundity and can be trusted to guide our spiritual journey.

Jesus

This matter should not be approached as if it were a debate; rather, can you explain why you have come to what you have said about dreams?

SOCRATES

You reason well, Jesus, so let me set out the relation between dreams and the mind. First, the communications of the Mind have that sole purpose. Once it is known that dreams carry these themes, it is not possible to ignore them. These messages in our dreams repeat the theme that in accepting a fundamentally flawed idea of Reality, we suffer terrible consequences. For, to be deceived and ignorant of the meaning of these messages always brings misfortune. No one would consciously choose to believe in these false images of Reality if they were shown what is true.

JESUS

So here you set forth something wondrous and moving. Could you say more about the drama of dreams? I find that very interesting and wonder about the depth that can be present in dreams.

SOCRATES

The drama of dreams nearly always presents an image or symbol of the Self that is the root cause of our unsuspected problems. The drama of the dream captures a vivid presentation of the drama of one's problems. The task is to turn the vision of man around from his unsuspected beliefs about himself and Reality to the mystery of our existence. This blindness is called "having and being possessed by one's problem." A problem is a false belief about oneself that is assumed by the believer to be the truth. The false belief's existence is entirely unsuspected, and it takes on the character of being obviously true. These false beliefs were concluded from early life experiences when the child exhibited a sense of freedom and openness as they violated the boundaries of the family clan identity. For the child to accept the false as true requires the parental figures had to appear as knowing, caring, and sincere, or it would never have been believed.

Within dreams, there are high and low states of mind. The high and profound states of mind are most often ignored or dismissed by dreamers. However, if they can be dwelt upon and explored with skill, it is possible for the dreamer to realize the depth and profound nature of these states of mind. Indeed, if the conditions are present, it is very possible for the dreamer to be brought to realize that they are experiencing different stages of enlightenment. Among such experiences are those enlightenment experiences of the most brilliant light of Being, or the Idea of the Good. The analysis of the dream not only can bring this to light, but the dreamer will be brought to experience that enlightenment state during the analysis itself. Indeed, that is a higher order, since it includes a deep understanding along with it.

JESUS

Now that is truly remarkable. What name do you give to this kind of learning? I have heard a bit about your dream work and would like to know how you and your followers name what you do.

SOCRATES

Philosophical midwifery is the name of this method true philosophers use to overcome ignorance and to gain the wisdom that enlightens every man. It offers the paradigm for understanding human problems and the way to the perfection of the Soul. It is through it we discover and can confirm for ourselves that we are not alone.

JESUS

Is it usual or rare to bring dreamers to recognize these experiences as enlightenment experiences in their dreams?

SOCRATES

Among those who have an interest in exploring the Self, a fair number of dreamers have been brought to realize not only enlightenment experiences, but also the meaning of them in terms of their spiritual life. It is all a part of being a philosopher. My art of philosophical midwifery, as I have said, has its parallels with my mother's art, for I should add that she was known as one of those who mastered midwifery for women who were pregnant. Her art reached a high point since could detect very early signs of pregnancy, assist women in the trials and difficulties of childbirth, and after assisting in the birth, judge if the birth was a true and noble birth or if it should be abandoned. She knew something few midwifes ever get to know; she knew what kind of relationships would prove to be beneficial and which not. My art parallels hers in every way, except I bring to birth ideas, not children.

Jesus

I find that very important, because the skill the maker of dreams must possess to achieve these profound goals is amazing to contemplate. It is, indeed, a fine art to know which love unions will bring the rewards of intimacy, and which not.

Socrates

Very true, Jesus, it is a noble art. And in respect to dreams, I would say that the total number of dreams appearing to all living beings throughout all time is a staggering number. These dreams always come to those who grasp for meaning on some higher level. The dreams bring a unique object of learning for the dreamer to comprehend. For a dream to be able to be uniquely meaningful to each soul, it must have an image of the Self that the dreamer can identify with. It must have a drama that has an analogue with an unsuspected problem the dreamer is facing in his present world, and the solution of one's unsuspected problem must be central to the spiritual life.

Yes, I can see why you say that, Socrates.

SOCRATES

I am pleased to hear that. Now, since we are not aware of the masks we wear we also do not realize that the way we function to achieve our goals may defeat our best efforts and bring us ruin. We are urged to carefully set before us the most ideal circumstances and then to devote ourselves to the mastery of some profound task such as reading one of the works of the sages.

SOCRATES

Yes, you are correct in seeing that, Jesus. For the art behind this ability to surface an unsuspected problem is a spiritual knowledge that benefits and nurtures the soul. We call the maker of dreams the "Dream Maker." After we bring to light these profound dreams, we often burn a stick of incense to honor that maker of dreams. It is from these kinds of reflections that we can say we are part of a caring and intelligible cosmos that we participate in and can become in union with.

JESUS

So you have brought many to recognize we are part of a caring cosmos, and you demonstrate that in many ways, but it seems the most direct way is through dreams. Surely it is a personal way to bring people to see that we participate in Mind seeking to know the Mind. You know, of course, that the idea of participation is alien to theistic systems of belief. I have learned much about it and would love to hear what you think of this idea, Socrates.

SOCRATES

Yes, much has been said about the idea of participation. For all the words that have been spun creating this fabric of ideas, it has huge holes in it. Let me share with you the mystery. The ideas that can be inferred from that experience of divine luminosity we call Ideas.

Thus, in beholding that Light, we can infer from it a set of Ideas as the primary causes of the manifestation in our world. Becoming receptive to such influences opens one to it. This openness is the condition for a kind of goodness to emerge that directly assists one to grasp and understand these very Ideas. It has a force that shapes the soul for that vision. Surely you would agree that the word that describes a goodness that reaches out to all and that benefits each uniquely is the name for Providence. The goodness is essential to the divine luminosity as its vitality and joyous way of being unveils what is noble and true. It is with reference to this experience that one can recognize images of Reality from mere shadows of Reality. So it is one thing to behold the Good as the divine luminosity, and quite another thing to go from that to the Good itself.

We could make a similar contrast between those who have only experienced divine luminosity and those who have encountered the Good itself. If one has encountered the state of the One itself, it would be impossible to believe the Good, or the One, is the Creator God. For if it can be described as having a particular mode of existence, as well as a power, and an activity of any kind, it certainly couldn't be said to be the Good or the One.

Jesus

Another of your thoughtful remarks that brought me to wonder; however, I am still interested in these holes you just mentioned that the idea of participation has.

Socrates

It is good that you reminded me of that idea. Consider that I could use any of the principal ideas we just mentioned that were inferred from that majestic experience. So I shall use the idea of Beauty. Beauty is encountered in our natural world in a wide variety of experiences. For all the multiplicity of instances, we recognize something similar, or we wouldn't say we experience beauty. The source of those experiences is an encounter with Beauty itself. I offer no explanation of how this takes place; it simply is. I lack any explanation for this. It is a profound mystery. I lack a theory of participation, yet I say it happens. It happens; it is the way of divine things.

Jesus

If it happens as you suggest, then how is it related to higher principles? Let me put it another way. Would you say that the principles of your midwifery are the same or different from what we call the higher Intelligible principles?

Socrates

You have a good question there, and it does take seeing a similarity between things not normally seen as such. Consider, the principles of midwifery are like a shadow, as it were, of the Intelligible principles, and it is the avenue through which further insight into this higher source can become available to us. Along the way, there is a learning of the language of the Dream Maker. It is this kind of reflection that is present in both our midwifery and dreams that naturally turns back upon that from which it derived its own existence. Clearly, this similar dynamic that midwifery reflects is an imitation of the reversion upon that from which we have derived the source of our very existence.

Jesus

So you are expressing the idea of cause through these explorations.

Socrates

Yes, you are correct about that. For the Soul, or the Self, proceeds from itself as a cause since it unknowingly framed its unique false belief and role from very early transmission scenes. Having been the unique source of its own pathologos, it has the power and the capability of dissolving it. We call any false belief about the Self a "pathologos," or a sick logos. The kind of understanding that surfaces these sick beliefs and confirms their dissolution through testing for their presence in experience is a more profound experience of the understanding. It is an experience that is parallel to scenes of its imposition or origin. Recognizing the falsity of the pathologos bequeaths a benefit to the soul. For the resulting change in the soul reveals that the pathologos was not essential to its nature. A higher state of mind that had been blocked by the transmission of the pathologos can now be resumed. The soul can now freely engage itself in the further development of its more awakened Self.

Jesus

So an analogy became an allegory, and what you have just said returns it to its analogical mean like a perfect pearl hidden within an oyster's shell. Would you also offer another account of dreams and how they relate to your idea of the soul and to philosophy?

Socrates

In philosophical midwifery, for a dream to be able to be uniquely meaningful to each soul, it must have an image of the Self that the dreamer can identify with. It must have a drama that has an analogue with an unsuspected problem the dreamer is facing in his present world, since the solution of one's unsuspected problem must be central to one's spiritual life.

The source of the perfection of the Soul lies in the discovery of its own higher reason for existing. This reason springs from an intelligence that it also shares in, for it reverts upon itself at the very moment that it opens a more profound state of mind called the twilight of the experience of the Intelligence.

The very way it proceeds in this process of dialogue is the exercise of a cognitive faculty we call the understanding, and it culminates in the openness that is the shadow of the openness and freedom of a clear and pure Mind functioning. This philosophical way of proceeding highlights its very mode of existing and in that turning about, which is an *ousia* movement, it reverts upon the Intelligence. Thus, this way of understanding unites into a oneness, and in doing so it returns it to its natural source, the Intelligence; as a result, what before was a scattered multiplicity without coherence and integrity becomes a set of ideas linked together with an inner coherence that to grasp requires the Intellect be put into play. The moment of insight reveals its mode of existence has a higher and more profound mode of existence, and since it lacks any image of oneself, we can say that it ushers in a dawning realization that the soul is not subject to time.

Yes, these kinds of experiences prepare the mind for more penetrating insight into our mode of existence, into its more profound way of functioning, and that it has a power capable of reaching to what is most divine. This activity the soul experiences is in time, but in these states of mind, it steps out of that temporal passing phase of being and enters into the timelessness of Reality. So this is why it can be said that the soul's activity is in time as its existence is timeless, or eternal. We could conclude that since it reverts upon itself in its activity, and since it is also recursive in respect to its existence, it is self-constituted. This idea of being self-constituted means all its functions, its mode of being, and its power and activity are all within itself, and it stands independent of anything else, so that we can say it is self-constituted.

Jesus

You do your work both in private and before others. I wondered what effect you saw it had on those who witnessed these philosophical midwife discussions or dream work?

SOCRATES

In the dream analysis sessions, those present gain the insight that we can all share in being witnesses to understanding another's problem. This sharing of a personal problem with others is evidence that this kind of cognitive activity brings a kinship and benefit with and to other minds. Even though I offer this as an explanation, it does nothing to remove its mystery.

JESUS

There you go again, Socrates, making a mystery of what you made obvious. All you need to say is that we are part of a spiritual Cosmos and this is the work of the divine. Still, I do see why you say it is a mystery. Shall we now turn to Aristotle?

SOCRATES

Aristotle rejects this idea of participation, and in its place he says that all ideas, like Beauty, have their essence only in the particular thing that has it. There is no such thing, he argues, as Beauty itself. All things that have become beautiful had that power to be so within themselves. The power to be able to do this lies within each thing, and so it is called its potential. The expression of this power in each thing is called its motion, or way of becoming.

JESUS

Very clever, to avoid your idea of participation, he created a new language. It has the image of something coming out of Nature.

SOCRATES

Yes, it is derived from the study of Nature. When viewed only from the empirical view the actualization can be viewed as the power of Nature. There is no participation in the Intelligible; Nature surfaces its forms. The underlying Reality of the visible forms resides in its substance. Thus, whatever growth and development anything has in Nature is because it contains within it the potential to be it. Aristotle is guided by the analogy: As a potential is to its actualization, so a seed is to its fullest flowering. The flowering is its form. Whatever exists is a unity of its form and its substance. The substance of all is a separate thing having its own existence. Substance resides within each thing's form and is itself unknown.

Jesus

Curious and more curious it is. Where does he say all this is going? Is there any goal or purpose to the whole of this?

Socrates

Once you ask where all this individual actualization of its potential is going, the answer is: nowhere special. There is no divine plan it is working through. What sets off all motion is called an unmoved mover. However, this unmoved mover is not aware of itself working towards any goal or fulfilling any promise, or itself being the blissful goal of intelligent beings.

Jesus

Well, that means it is not a God at all. How can this unmoved mover be a God if it neither has a purpose nor any interaction with man? He surely closed the door on any discussion of your Greek Gods or the Intelligible realm, didn't he? He saw so much in Nature; yet saw so little of the Intelligible that we can wonder about the nature of his soul.

Socrates

Yes, he did close the door. To open it is difficult yet simple. Those we call deniers deny the role of the mind. Paul and Aristotle are the deniers who created alternative systems to avoid the teaching of their teachers. As for Mark, he rejects Paul-the-denier, so we can also call him the denier of the denier.

Jesus

Socrates, you are among the noblest and wisest of teachers, and you know that your words were left to other interpreters who should have first experienced these sacred things before proclaiming what they thought was true.

Chorus

Here is another so-called analysis and it is as empty as empty can be. Analogies again—phooey on them! You can do anything with 'em and none of it can be confirmed. The cornerstone of Christianity, Paul, is dismissed with a few words. He is the one who made the resurrection perfectly clear. Wake up and look instead of shouting nonsense. First off, there was a resurrection. It is a simple fact, undeniable as it is. How can all those who witnessed it be wrong? Behind all your blah blah is nothing but a doubting Thomas.

As for Aristotle, that's easy. Once you realize all this talk about enlightenment will not save your soul, then you'll see the truth. Dump this philosophy and master nature. Mastering nature gives you power to manipulate her, torture her to get her secrets out of her; that's what experiments are, simply torture. What you really need to do is to drop your philosophy. Then you'll see you only need a practical approach that is free of all the ambiguity of your philosophy. What's that? That is Aristotle. You don't need anything more once you've got your faith. You need faith because of the failure of understanding; we are too weak for the task, and that's all.

Anti-Chorus

Now it is your turn to listen. It is true that analysis is empty. All you need to know is what it is empty of. Go back again to what has been said. See if this analysis is empty of interpretations that are foreign to the work. It is as painful to realize that you have been persuaded to believe what is manifestly false as it is to realize that you have undergone a suffering of your own making. Wake up from your own folly. Put aside these deniers of truth and seek your freedom in the truths you discover about yourself. Face it, you are afraid to look at yourself.

SOCRATES

You mentioned that some of the gospels were unearthed in Egypt; did any continue your work? If so, they are likely to fit into one of our divisions.

JESUS

Yes, many works were recovered. Many of them follow the way of Knowledge as the way to salvation. They share a view of God that sets the conditions for their system. The Gospel of Thomas, and the Secret Book of Thomas, and even of Judas, were among the major works recovered.

SOCRATES

If there were once many texts, shall I assume many were tossed into the flames? Book burning has a long history, doesn't it? When were the chosen ones selected?

JESUS

It was 300 years after my departing that the Church selected the popular works of the New Testament. The rest were destroyed, or so it was thought. They chose only those that could support their drive to dominate and control their people within a church system. Since the Gnostic works stress the way of Knowledge, there is no need for faith as the road to salvation, nor a need for the church.

Some fifty have been recovered and among them, five are considered most significant.

SOCRATES

What kinship do these have? I do wonder what made them special and if these works fit into one or another of our divisions.

JESUS

These are the works that cite me as being present as the speaker, and the others mentioned are among my circle of apostles. I am shown to be continuing my work, with Matthew as my recorder, teaching to a select audience. They draw from my analogies, allegories, parables, and metaphors and add their special differences.

The Book of Thomas is said to be the one most akin to me. Thomas lays emphasis upon divine luminosity as being inherent within all, as the ideal of my teachings, and the practice to follow. In his repeating the theme of the Delphic Oracle's "Know Thyself" and linking it with the divine luminosity, he brings us together. Without that most splendid theme, know thyself, there would be no philosophy. He presents me filled with that light that is the light from the Father. He called those enlightened who are filled with that light, since they have that light within themselves. These are the ones that are said to have gained the saving Knowledge that marks them as Gnostic thinkers. The idea of the Kingdom of God, like in Mark, is to be experienced here and now. Clearly there is a difference, since there is no mention of the arrest, trial, crucifixion, and resurrection.

SOCRATES

This is a very important philosophic addition to the Gospel, Jesus, since Thomas is linking Plato to your teaching. However, there is no room for dreams here, is there? He is conscious of continuing

your work just as Plato did with me. He looks like a category four
to me. What do you think?

JESUS

Yes, he does that very thing. The additional strength is that he
was my twin and there is much we share.

SOCRATES

They both go beyond the four Gospels and Paul. Thomas advances
a synthesis or unity of both of our traditions. He must be a new
member of our class. Now what of James?

JESUS

He is at the other extreme, of course, from the Book of Thomas
and the Gospel of Thomas. The sharp contrasts they include are the
apocalyptic themes, which are repeated in those other gospels. The
Secret Book of James repeats the passion themes and presents itself
as filling in the teachings that were absent during my ministry. The
teaching given to James and Peter is called the revelation of James.
The new teaching brings to light the theme of enlightenment, for
he says to be saved, one needs to "Know Thyself." Importantly,
the Gnostic John introduces fundamental Hellenic philosophical
terms into his work; he uses them for his explanations into the
divine luminosity, and in doing so, links his work to the Hellenic
spiritual tradition.

So it is that he retains the core beliefs and continues Thomas'
synthesis of our traditions. He keeps both, and that makes him a
member of a new class.

SOCRATES

With that I can agree. We are adding members to our class and
that is a good sign we are still making some progress with our task.

Clearly, the necessity of "knowing thyself" is the most fundamental of ideas in our traditions. It is the true mark of the true Hellenic Logos. All my philosophy mirrors that idea, and when it is ignored, what remains of it is a hollow empty system. Surely you agree that all the mysteries of our systems spin about the idea of the Self.

Jesus

What you say is true and needs to be said. In addition, we can say that among the Gnostic works, John's work opens with his account of his divine luminosity and his work includes an account of what can be learned from it. The ideas he brings into a unity include ideas like thought, after-thought, fate, perfect knowledge, mind, and the personification of Wisdom as Christ. The crisis man faces, for John, is his forgetfulness and passions. This is similar indeed to Plato, for his idea of forgetfulness is overcome with a knowledge anchored in the divine luminosity through its recovery in awakening and recalling one's inner vision. How this was practiced we do not know. There is no lack of philosophical themes, but there is a need for supporting literature to support its themes. He does not add any reference or practice of your kind of dream study.

Again, we find that John's account does not mention anything at all of the passion material nor any reference to the resurrection stories of the three New Testament Gospels.

Socrates

You end by seeing the link with the Hellenic tradition. However, what you present as an answer, we use as a departure point for understanding. Perhaps this is fundamental. To understand something, you need the necessary connecting ideas to explain it, or if one lacks those, the terms may live on as slogans without the understanding to comprehend their depth. Without these key terms, there is no way one can achieve an understanding of these kinds of teachings and experiences. These terms are Platonic and common to the Hellenic world, but they do not appear present in the Abrahamic traditions.

JESUS

Surely you know we have a different origin to our beliefs. We come from the seed of the Abrahamic tradition, not that of the Hellenes.

SOCRATES

What do you include in this idea of the Abrahamic traditions?

JESUS

The Abrahamic traditions, Judaism, Christianity, and Islam, are religions that require faith or belief as the fundamental commitment. Each has a set of holy texts that reveal the nature of God, creation, man's role in it, and his true destiny. These traditions are strangers to your kind of thinking.

SOCRATES

This, of course, accounts for the Gnostic Book of John being more accessible and favored among those attracted to the use of reason as a guide in their spiritual quest. I am interested in this work, but right now it confirms that the Book of John and Gospel of Thomas support Mark's rejection of Paul.

JESUS

Yes, and during that early period when both Mark and the Book of Thomas were being circulated, it was possible to accept Thomas and be a follower of mine while ignoring the story of the passion, trial, crucifixion, and resurrection. Recall that I said that Thomas calls himself my twin and by that he announces a priority over all others. For since he was appointed to my inner circle, and being my brother, he should have known my end, should he not?

In linking the luminosity to knowing the Self and to Wisdom, he looks much like he is more akin to you than to me, or our differences narrow. However, he assigns the fundamental cause for our ignorance as indulging in sexuality. I know you differ from him on that very point.

SOCRATES

Yes, he can find the divine hidden or absent in significant acts of mankind. I fathered my last son when I was about 70, having already had several sons. Shall I say something else is needed to explain man's ignorance?

JESUS

I have heard that you are a lover, a father, a warrior, and are said to be among the most wise.

SOCRATES

Now, to understand what blocks mankind from knowing himself may be a simple matter and yet it is a mystery to most. It is said that it is because man sins that he is blind to the goodness of the divine. I have an interest in this idea of sin and would like to learn more about it. We call it holding fast to a false belief as if it were true. It is an error, a mistake, and even something you don't even recognize as a mistake, yet it seems as if it is impossible to dismiss or avoid. Those that are impossible to avoid have become the subject of tragedy, the fatal flaw of the tragedian. So tell me, how does sin—as Thomas views it—keep one from the divine luminosity and knowing the Self?

JESUS

To answer that question, I will have to fill you in on the great sin, because for Thomas there is another greater kind of sin, and this one you are most likely to reject. The greater is if after hearing his teaching, you dismiss it, scorn it, and flee from it. For that dismissal, one descends into the depths of your Tartarus. The other, which is more pervasive and engulfs all of mankind, is sexual intercourse and passion. These teachings are told to Matthew by Thomas, and in his report I am seen as if I am instructing him.

SOCRATES

Right you are; I would reject the idea that love expressed through bodily desires is sin. Now those who are free of these two kinds of sin must reach the heavens; how is it described?

JESUS

Thomas says that those who reach this exalted state become united with the most holy King of Kings. He goes on to say, however, that it is essential to "know thyself." Now, what questions do you have for me?

SOCRATES

It is curious that he could believe that after coming to "know thyself," one would be celibate. It also lacks a description, since being united with the King of Kings is hardly a description. Further, it is difficult to believe that these stories of the resurrection, final judgment, and the apocalypse were known by Thomas and the others and were simply ignored. Could Thomas, in writing about you, have known these things and simply chose to ignore them? For if he knowingly rejected that, we must ask what higher purpose could he have had in mind when he skipped over these events in his account?

JESUS

You continue your reflections, determined to seek out the Truth. Now, you are in the same boat as I am since your question and doubts have turned us both around. As you know, Thomas, the twin, was my brother and among my followers he was closest to me; we drank from the same sacred source. It is true that his Gospel had no arrest, no trial, no crucifixion, and, of course, no resurrection. These four major events are not part of Thomas, and neither are they in the common material shared by Matthew and Luke, and that is called "Q." This material of "Q" is dated earlier than either Gospel since it has been dated around 50 AD. Clearly, these four events were added later to the account of the gospels.

These additions sprung from the transfiguration experience that Mark introduced into his Gospel and the other two Gospels shared it, but the transfiguration experience is not in the Gospel of John. My ministry was said to have taken a severe change after that dialogue between Moses, Elijah, and me. For surely, as interpreters fly in different directions, so this signals a basic change in my presumed ministry.

Socrates

If Thomas didn't get the whole of it right, what of the work of James?

Jesus

The Gnostic Gospel of James won favor among those who sought an entry into the Kingdom of God through understanding parables. His way was to bring people to the Kingdom by urging them to become perfect and to be filled with the spirit. He stressed the importance of experiencing the divine light and urged his followers to understand not only the parables but also what the light is.

Socrates

Yes, the most brilliant light of Being is also the goal of many of our seekers. Does he advance other ideas?

Jesus

Yes, Socrates, and he does continue to preach about Satan, as does James, and they both need to believe in the cross and in my death. From this, we can say that he continues several core beliefs of the canonical gospels. Curious, is it not, Socrates, that in stressing the need to remember, both while awake and asleep, that he becomes part of your tradition? Is this an attempt to bridge or unite two different traditions?

Socrates

Could be, but I would need to know more about how his followers carried out that practice because it has echoes back to the importance of remembering and, possibly, dream work. It looks like he adds to the work and retains some of the core beliefs. From this, I can conclude that he is another Gnostic gospel writer who rejects Paul. However, while I say this, I am not at all sure I can say what the core saving belief of Paul's teaching is.

Jesus

The saving belief that Paul thought was essential for the spiritual life was his idea of justification by faith. He says that since the Son of God died for your sins, it is in your faith that your sins will be forgiven. He died for your sins to be forgiven. Surely you are likely to reject this idea, but it is simply that whatever the sin or fault that is committed, it can be wiped clean because of my death. He sees my death as a sacrifice for all man's sins and this, of course, was simply incompatible with Mark's account of my death and my last words. Surely, if one experiences an abandonment it cannot turn that into one's sacrifice.

Socrates

I find your remark important without fully understanding it. Could you explain it for me?

Jesus

Mark has it all, and he says it simply. When one cries aloud, "Why hast thou abandoned me?" it announces that the former relation with God has been forsaken. Even the term carries a heavy weight since it also includes within itself the idea that God should not have done so. To abandon anything means it has been rejected totally. In sacrificing, one also gives up some treasure, but does so voluntarily to honor someone. Under the stress of abandonment, one experiences rejection and loneliness while with sacrifice one experiences righteousness and peace in their soul.

Socrates

To see the folly of a decision that seemed to have been the mark of truth upon it and base one's fate upon it only to see you are wrong is what we Hellenes call a true tragedy.

Jesus

You are too quick to come to your conclusion, Socrates. While it is true these Gospels agree that the transfiguration experience shows that I did identify with the fate of Elijah and so took upon myself the role of the Son of David, what you ignore is that scene where I am described as crying aloud, and in that sense there is no realization I was wrong.

Socrates

Then it cannot be a tragedy, can it? For, the hero must realize that he was wrong and that his whole way of being was wrong. What then?

Jesus

After the transfiguration, in Mark I am said to be acting out Elijah's role so that the scripture can be fulfilled. Clearly, Socrates, that was the plan in my going to Jerusalem. What other conclusion can be drawn than that the drama of Elijah ends in disaster?

So, Paul takes abandonment as a sacrifice which, of course, is to deny that my mission was to act out the passion story that was linked to the image and teachings of David. Paul had a vision which was that all mankind must become a more inclusive Judaism that brings together the circumcised and those circumcised in the spirit.

SOCRATES

Then all of mankind would become Pauline Jews, wouldn't they?

JESUS

To ignore these things means they never occurred, or that Thomas chose to ignore these very profound and startlingly important events. Which would you say is more likely?

SOCRATES

Your question raises one we often reflect upon. It deals with the nature of what is to be called likely and what not. Thomas' book and the gospels present extremely different views of your work. How do you understand such differences?

JESUS

Obviously, in writing his work, he singled out what he regarded as true about my ministry and what he thought did not happen, he ignored. So, we can say that with them all, can't we?

SOCRATES

It could not be made clearer than in this way: Thomas ignored Paul's claim that you are the only Son of God. I come to one conclusion if none of the Gnostic authors, nor Mark, assign you that title. So then, while the Jesus of Mark rejects the teachings of Paul, he still includes the core beliefs of the Abrahamic tradition. However, in Mark's account, did your last words mean that there was no saving God and in that he rejected the model of sacrifice? Is the core belief of your tradition Abraham's willingness to do as his God commanded, and that was the beginning of the model for sacrifice?

Jesus

Yes, in a way it was, and in another way, not. The model such believers act out can be easily perceived. Look closely at the roots of their teaching and you'll surface their problematic model. How did the God of Abraham choose those who were to be his people? They are the ones following the model of Abraham. As Abraham so feared not obeying the commands of his God that he was willing to sacrifice his first son, so too his followers obey his laws and become his people.

So pleased was this God with Abraham's willingness to sacrifice his son that he formed a clan of worthy, fierce believers from Abraham's descendants. For these are called the chosen people. They were given the right to conquer and possess the land of others. They have been told that their God will curse those who curse them, and those they bless he will bless. This God became a servant of his people. So this God announced he would do unto others what others do to them. This God becomes his people's ally and pours wrath upon their enemies. This God becomes a people's God whose highest vision is that they become the rulers of mankind.

Socrates

Then what they will act out is not their will, but only what is consistent with Abraham's fearful legacy from his wrathful God.

JESUS

It is likely that here you will see a loss of freedom, but I will see conformity to divine rule. To be willing to stay within those limits is to be a child of God.

SOCRATES

I see, then, that in accepting the creed, it imposes limits on what can be questioned. One pays a bitter price for believing truth can be reached by sanctifying the shadows in the cave of belief. Doing so is to celebrate blindness as if it were sight. Thus, in this way, they sacrifice any meaningful exploration of the elements of theology, or metaphysics. Putting limits on the Mind is to sacrifice the Mind. If this is common to the Abrahamic religions, then they are in conflict with understanding, reason and the use of the Intellect or Mind.

The reduction of God to serve and function as a servant for his people is no longer to have a God. Notice, then, that Mark's Jesus hoped to force God's hand and save him from the cross, and in doing so, his followers would become another people, another tribe of chosen people. Paul's theme saved this ideal by the belief in your resurrection.

What is this but the sacrifice of the fullest scope of the Mind for membership in a clan that is protected by their God?

JESUS

I see that you use the idea of limit frequently, Socrates. Clearly, you are saying, are you not, that while those who become a follower of Abraham gain an identity and power, they do so at the cost of the use of the higher functions of the mind. You call that a necessary limit to their being. This is quite a claim. How do you intend to defend it? If you have reasons I would like to hear them.

SOCRATES

True it is because it will take several steps in reasoning to realize the grounds for my making that claim.

JESUS

I would appreciate if you were to take me through such steps, Socrates.

SOCRATES

Among groups of people, is it not true that there are some who have created spiritual systems that depend upon their God's will to direct them in their everything they do? And, by contrast, there are others that, while they also include the idea of God in their spiritual system, they depend upon their own teachings and efforts to direct them in everything they think and do.

JESUS

Yes, I can see why you say that.

SOCRATES

From this separation into these two groups we can say that the first group is other than the second, can we not? Or, that they are other than the others?

JESUS

Yes, to that too.

SOCRATES

What separates these others from the others is that they have a different idea of how to relate to their God since in the first group they must obey and serve the will and interests of their God. This idea is one of master and servant, and since to serve their God they must conquer lands and subject all to the will of their God, that means that they sacrifice their own goals and interests for the sake of the whole of which they are parts.

JESUS

Again, I can see where you are going, and it does sound like a master-slave relationship, and if so they must hide that from themselves.

Each individual within this group uses their mind only within the limits of what is commanded by their God and they consider all else as secondary; all else can also be ignored and considered to be without merit.

JESUS

Yes, that does seem to follow.

Then these followers share a commonness with each other and know that they differ from that other group who seek the direction of their spiritual path within themselves and do so through the use of the mind. They must stand alone from those who use the mind to know the mind; otherwise they would abandon their God and seek to follow the command to Know Thyself. They must remain within their self-imposed limits and know that even among others of their group they have betrayed their self to follow their God's will. So, in relation to each other and within themselves they know they have sacrificed themselves in obedience to their God. Among themselves they experience this tension since they are like themselves and like each other and on the other hand they experience that they are unlike those members of that other system and suffer that loss while keeping it from one another.

JESUS

I do think that what you say can be said.

SOCRATES

Then, even though they accept this limitation they still can function with a partial logos and achieve everyday goals which, of course, must be consistent with the demands of their God. They must agree not to free themselves nor enter into the logos so they are free to master the everyday world and ignore the further most reach of the mind, or else they will lose what they have treasured the most, a group identity with their God. They participate in limit while their own spirit is unlimited since it willingly plays whatever subordinate role is their fate.

JESUS

Now, this is more difficult to agree with, but at this point I have nothing to oppose it.

SOCRATES

And, if one's way of being can be descend from one's model then as the God of Abraham was willing to murder his son as a sacrifice to his God so the followers of Abraham must be willing to murder others to fulfill the will of their God. We can add that as one identifies with one's self-image, these followers of Abraham must act according to that image, and so they have a fixed way of being that limits and blocks their spiritual development.

JESUS

I would not have expressed that in such terms, nor do those followers of Abraham picture themselves in that way, but I do see why you use that language to describe them.

SOCRATES

Very good, Jesus, you gave birth to just what I expected from you.

SOCRATES

Putting the matter that way offers me a way to explore another parallel. For now we can ask, "What was ignored or added as it moved from Thomas?" Clearly, since Truth is what we seek, it would be important to also look behind the words and seek to identify what springs from those words.

JESUS

Yes, seeking Truth brings one to face the mystery hidden behind the spiritual quest.

SOCRATES

It is said that when the mysteries become obvious then the many are seen as reflections of that which is itself a reflection.

JESUS

And, Socrates, the many can only be entertained, not taught the mysteries. They don't seek to understand these sacred things; either they stand in awe of them, or they simply ignore them.

SOCRATES

Your words reflect the teachings of the sages, Jesus, but my way is to show that those who possess skills like those who are tanners, smiths and shoemakers have principles that underlie their skills that are not different from the spiritual principles of philosophy. Recall that my philosophy starts with the fundamental principle that as Heaven is to Earth so model is to copy.

It is from their own work that I mold images of excellence since these contain all that man needs to become noble and good. As I explore these ideas, I reflect upon the role of the Gods that they have heard many times and weave my philosophy around them. Consider my analogy: as Theseus must slay the Minotaur, so the philosopher must slay death. As with you, this was a central teaching that I often repeated. I stressed how to separate the soul from the body and so experience dropping dead before one drops dead.

JESUS

You awaken your people to the mystery of life and death by awakening their fears and hopes about life and death. You lift their everyday experience to the level of the profound. You allegorize their myths to show parallels with the spiritual plane. But did your Plato make as clear as he could have what you were doing? Is your teaching for all mankind or only for the Hellenes? I say that because Hellenic myths fall on deaf ears in the lands of Judaea.

SOCRATES

You are correct in raising that point, Jesus. My interpreter, Plato, gave only one sentence to describe this spiritual practice of dying. He left that teaching without explaining how one must gather together the soul from body when it is separating itself outside of the body. Is it a gradual process or attained instantaneously? In missing that key factor, the understanding of this spiritual practice was left undeveloped. For if the attainment is only seen altogether and at once, then all the processes may lead to it but are far different from it, just as understanding differs from true Knowledge. Those who brought Hellenic thought to other traditions but ignored this practice, ignored my essential practice of what it is to be a true philosopher.

JESUS

My ministry, like yours, has waited for someone who can see what we have seen, and can understand what we have come to know. It is natural that we both have had many interpreters, but among them some of the most superficial have been protected and maintained by authorities. These are the ones who know better but are afraid of challenging a traditional misunderstanding. There is one work we mentioned, the Gospel of John. He started in a most beautifully profound way but lost his thread and his work ended in shatters. We both know that this can always be expected, but these authorities lead many followers into the absurd and hide from them what they most need to know.

SOCRATES

Yes, authorities have conspired to reduce wisdom to image-thinking belief. Could you share what John said because I have yet to hear about this.

JESUS

Surely, the true mystery is always with us, in front of us, and eternally present to us, but we cannot believe what our experience reports to us. John caught a glimpse of it in his Gospel and said it with charm but lost his vision soon after and descended into Paul's vision. I can recall what John actually said in the beginning of his Gospel. He said it well: "All things came to be through the Self and apart from the Self not one thing came to be. In Self was life and this life was the light of human beings; and since the light shines in the darkness, but the darkness cannot understand the Self. A human being came to be, sent on a mission from God, John was the name given by the Self. This very Self came to bear witness in order to give evidence about the light in order that all may have belief through Self. That very Self was not the light, but Self came in order to give evidence about the light." So, he started as some racers do as they start with a flash of speed only to lose their breath after going a short distance.

SOCRATES

When those few realize what we have said, we can easily see what they will demand, can't we? For, surely they will raise the cry for further teachings of the Self.

They will demand from their priests and ministers insights into the Self, into the Logos, and for an understanding of these ideas so that they can continue the work we have become a part of. However, where could those churchmen direct their followers except to our philosophy?

Jesus

They will end their past struggles and begin anew in the life of the spirit.

Socrates

Then we must face a curious problem since we both have experienced its tragic side. Why is the traditional view of both of our teachings so popular? We both have seen our teachings descend into this popular view, but how do you understand this transformation?

Jesus

What most want to believe they wait to insert into whatever teaching is current. My followers are attracted to the teachings of Paul and for you it is Aristotle.

It does not matter how they differ; the result is the same. They both fear the experience of the Self, of the Mind, and the Logos, which is, of course, the experience of the divine. That's all. It is that simple.

So, we can say that our Gnostic thinkers are in agreement with the ideas of the Self that we just noted in the Gospel of John, but they do not touch upon your essential practice of dying and death, for there is no greater mystery for mankind than the meaning of one's own death.

Socrates:

With the Self there goes faith and doubt since Self existence is obvious though mysterious, and doubt assumes a Self that doubts.

JESUS

So you say our Gnostic thinkers brought your ideas along with them, but not your essential practice, for there is no greater mystery for man than death.

SOCRATES

The recent interest among those who have survived death, what they call near-death experiences, sheds more light on this, doesn't it? For surely, Jesus, they have brought many to realize there is a cosmic integrity to our Cosmos. The fears that theistic religions pour down on their believers are not experienced upon death. A new possibility beyond these church teachings may arise. They have learned through these experiences that we are all here to learn and benefit one another.

JESUS

Learning from one another, you say, is important, and if I am to agree with you, we would need our interpreters to leave to their followers some practice that can achieve that lofty goal.

SOCRATES

Correct you are, Jesus, some profound spiritual experiences develop by themselves, others require learning. Some teachers offer freely what they have learned, others, like Plato in his dialogues, describe very profound experiences, without discussing how these states are to be realized. Plato stresses the role of dreams in the life of the philosopher but says nothing about how to understand dreams. He may actually be ignorant of this, since he fails to understand the dream Zeus sent to Agamemnon.

JESUS

Yes, Socrates, I experienced the same. I had stressed the need to experience and understand exalted states of mind, the Kingdom of God, and experiences of divine luminosity, but none of my inter-preters explained the nature of each, or how to go from the one to the other. Recall that when Mark explores the experience of divine luminosity, he adds a dialogue that took place between Moses, Elijah, and myself. The meaning of these events becomes the subject not of reflection, but of finding some meaning behind the drama Mark attributed to me.

Socrates

If that dialogue surfaces I would certainly like to hear of it. I would also like to learn the role that one called John the Baptist played in your ministry.

Jesus

John the Baptist announced me but what he did, I didn't do. For while he preached a baptism for the repentance for the forgiveness of sins, there is no example put forward that I did what the Baptist did.

Socrates

Yes, I can say the same. My teacher was said to be Diotima from Mantineia. Plato, in his *Symposium*, has me recalling the steps lead-ing to a vision of the perfection of Beauty, to Truth itself. Truly, it is a work of art. He brings the role of personification, myth, mean analogies, models of love, and even includes a spiritual practice to reach that vision. He was bold enough to say that here is a philosophy that can rival Homer and Hesiod. He adds that the experience of Truth or Beauty is not final, but that it is penultimate, since after that magnificent experience, Diotima notes there is something still to be done. It is incomplete. She points to the need to go further and cultivate a true excellence, because that kind of excellence alone will bring one to the eternal and to become a friend of God. However, as we expect, she says nothing about the nature and kind of that excellence, nor what it would take to bring it to a level of completion. You and I would say that the excellence could only be reached by becoming Socratic, but it took later philosophers to make that point. The question is: should Plato have added that? Curious, isn't it?

JESUS

Yes, I do find that question curious. Would you say that those later philosophers discovered more about your way of being than those who were present about you? If so, why do we have to wait for later thinkers to see what was already there to be seen in the past? Shall we say that later philosophers' visions were not obscured by a need to add what they wanted to believe to what was being revealed? However, I wonder if another way of looking at this would be helpful.

SOCRATES

Are you still wondering about that possibility and have entered into silence? Is it possible that I detect you are a bit cautious about advancing this idea of yours?

JESUS

You are right on both accounts. I am left wondering if Plato's Socrates presented an idealized version of what he saw as your life and practice. Has it not been said that if you teach that kind of excellence, you become a friend of God, Socrates? Could it be that in the imitation of his Socrates, one can reach that kind of excellence?

SOCRATES

Interesting summary and questions you raise. Then those who followed him would have the task of finding within his writings a model for their own spiritual life.

Jesus

Since you caught my meaning, can you say how we ought to judge if any have reached that excellence?

Socrates

Yes, we can apply Plato's own test. Those who have ascended and known the nature of the True Realities and of the Good, having returned to the cave, they can now see a thousand times better and know both what the images are and what they are images of. These images are what man takes as reality, and they permeate his thoughts, and dreams. Surely, realizing this as the way in which the Mind communicates to each and prepares one for vision is the essence of the noble pursuit of philosophy.

Jesus

Well said, Socrates, well said.

Chorus

Hear this foolishness and laugh out loud. There is no way to understand dreams. Excellence is nothing special. All you have to do is see what is accepted as excellence and compete against it only if you have to. Just ignore all this because Reality is what you make of it. There is no Reality lying out there to be seen. These guys want to say they have a double vision. They see what we see and in the same seeing, they claim to see a Reality different from what we see. Take a look. There is only one Reality and that's what you piece together after you experience whatever you experience. What could be more laughable than to read gospels that have been thrown out? Trash in, trash out, it's that simple.

Anti-Chorus

Why do you have to scream? From where does this loud boasting come? Are you trying to convince yourself? You are either right or wrong; that's all. Take the risk, use your Mind or rave against it. Fill your life with empty pleasures and ignore the challenge to see if there really is meaning to be realized. Go ahead and take the challenge. What do you have to lose by the effort? Just one thing, and that's your own cowardice in facing this very challenge.

JESUS

Yes, that would be good. I admired the skill you displayed in your attack against those fundamental Abrahamic religious ideas, and now I wonder if you are equally good at defending your own religious ideas. Can you pick a God from all the Gods of the Hellenes that was less irrational than we found in our exploration of Abraham's God? Which of the Gods in saving his people also offered a model for their sacrifice to God? Offer your defense and consider me as if I am the judge who will hear your case and decide if your defense has merit or not.

SOCRATES

And I admire your skill in setting out this next part of our exploration. Would you allow as the first stage of my defense that I first review a few fundamental ideas we have been using? I ask that because we need to understand how these two ideas, God and sacrifice, are to be understood in my defense before we introduce a Hellenic God.

JESUS

I will agree to that after you first explain why you need such an agreement before we start.

SOCRATES

How we each understand these two key ideas is so different that it would be best to show that their differences do not exclude them from being contrasted.

Jesus

Now, that is a good way to begin; go on, as you will.

Socrates

First, in the Hellenic world, there is only one theme playing itself out and that is the Will of Zeus expressing itself as Providence. The direct knowing of it may be beyond human reach, but the understanding of it is an essential task. Primarily, the principal Ideas inherent in the experience of Reality are personified as Gods. The total expression of all the primary ideas that can account for principles and conditions for the existence of the Cosmos constitute the catalogue of the characteristics of the Gods. The threefold condition for a God to be a God is that it expresses a mode of existence, a power, and an activity. Exploring these Hellenic Gods in this way brings clarity and levels of meaning within their mythology.

The movement from mythology to metaphysics shifts attention from metaphor to discovering rational structures and matching them with some mode of experience. The natural result of this kind of theology is that its parallel metaphysical expression of each of the Gods becomes a way of understanding the Gods within elements of theology.

Indeed, the One cannot be personified, nor can there be an image of it. It is the vital condition for there being Gods, and so, it is not a God among Gods. Even the earliest philosopher among the Hellenes calls it not a God but Mind. There are also those like Pythagoras and myself who say it is also called the One, or the Good, but its true name is the One Self.

Jesus

How did one of your philosophers express this way of viewing the Gods?

SOCRATES

There are several I could mention, but for this task, I think it best to call upon Sallustius or Proclus.

JESUS

The name Proclus is known here as a profound one. I'd choose whoever presented a way to understand the Olympian Gods.

SOCRATES

The Olympian Gods are a class of Gods within a matrix of Gods.

JESUS

Hold it for a moment. I would be amiss if I didn't stop you and ask about this matrix of Gods. Can you first explain how you are going to manage this exploration?

SOCRATES

I think it best if I describe the Soul's journey; that will present a picture of the causes and the conditions necessary for the ascent to the Good itself. The picture can go from the highest to the lowest or the reverse. Tell me which you would prefer.

JESUS

The lower to the higher.

SOCRATES

I will sketch out the journey in philosophical terms and then, by substituting the names of the Gods, you will understand the twelve worldly, or mundane, Gods and their hierarchical order.

JESUS

Now that is something I would like to see. Surely, the goal of life is to exhibit a mode of perfection through being what you truly are.

Socrates

I agree since the drive for perfection often begins after an encounter with works of beauty that could only have come into existence through the mastery of an art. Those who have such an encounter are then drawn to seek profound Truth. Such is the anagogic path.

Jesus

Before we explore the nature of these Gods, I would benefit by first learning what you see behind these terms that you use with such ease. What do you mean by the anagogic realm?

Socrates

Sure thing, it is my pleasure to explore that realm since it is so much akin to me. First, it is through the attraction and cultivation of harmony and rhythm that mankind first encounters the power of *ousia* through music and the experience of beauty. The attraction to beauty and harmony stirs the soul and awakens a love for the beautiful, and this power of *ousia* turns them about and pervades through their lives. The elevation of the soul is accompanied by a desire to understand and know the source of Beauty and Truth and this leads the soul to turn around and enquire philosophically, and it then becomes attracted to the dialectic, since this is what brings the soul to the Good itself. These three ways of being are called the anagogic triad.

Jesus

They are already turned around, are they not? Should we not first discuss what is behind this idea of the triadic order?

Socrates

Yes, that is a good idea. Let me ask you to consider: If there is a cause, must there also be the condition for a cause? For without the conditions, there would be no particular cause for anything to be.

The conditions for all principles and for living things to be must be prior to all else. However, for living things to be, there must be a power of life for them to be. Equally, having the power means, does it not, that their activity can proceed once living things have the power.

Jesus

I must say that I like those distinctions.

Socrates

Then we need another. Consider, must not each of these have a mode of existence?

Jesus

Sure thing, and that is as true as that the light proceeds from the existing sun; it must have a power to extend its rays throughout the heavens.

Socrates

Then we can expect each of these three fundamental ideas must have three modes of expressing themselves. Existence must have a mode of being, a power, and an activity, as power must have a mode of existing, a power, and an activity, and as activity must have its own mode of existing, its power, and its activity. However, to complete these, we need something that preserves these and maintains their existence and that also must have its existence, power, and activity.

Jesus

Now, are you going to say that for each of these there must be a God? That is astonishing!

Socrates

Tell me: What it is that you say is astonishing?

Jesus

It is beautiful in its simplicity, it is ordered in its structure, and it is what we must call rational.

Socrates

Yes, indeed, you have caught my meaning completely. I will set out the way they function and your task will be to give the particular God a name. I should first of all say that there are many Gods that function in many different orders and the one we agreed to discuss is called the mundane, worldly, or as I prefer to call them, the Gods of Nature. This is the realm of all living and intelligent beings. The Gods function in a hierarchical way to bring a full realization of the Truth to mankind.

The first of the Gods is the source of all that exists, and he is guided by divine Wisdom. It is through this that he takes care of all things both living and nonliving.

Second, there is a God who is the cause of *ousia's* power and motion, and it is through *ousia* that he rules over all motion and generation.

Another God is the divine power of *ousia* that proceeds to activity. It is this that inspires all generation in the psychical realm as well as inspires the soul to "Know Thyself."

There is a God that preserves the purity of *ousia* for all the Being of things and is the source of the stability of wholes.

There is a God that preserves lives through the inherent intelligence and energy of *ousia* and in this way sustains the power and purity of all Nature.

Again, another God guards the steadfast power of *ousia* to illuminate corporeal-formed bodies with power and strength, while giving the internal power of *ousia* a converting nature to those capable of receiving and turning about through it.

These Gods provide their guardians with the power to eternally maintain the order of Nature.

Among the Gods who are called vivific, there is the God that functions through the power of *ousia*. Through reverting upon itself, it elevates existence and in this way accounts for all things passing in and out of existence.

Another God is required for the power of *ousia* since the capacity for a divinity to turn upon itself is divine *ousia*.

Another God is needed to provide the condition for that power of *ousia* to extend to individual natures.

Last among this vivific triad is the God whose activity is to realize that activity of *ousia* in the birthing in all living things and to ensure there are principles for determining a true and noble birth from those empty of worth.

These Gods are the source of the life-giving or vivific power of *ousia* for all living things.

Among the last triads of Gods, which we call the anagogic, is the leader of individual souls to the profound activity of *ousia* in the philosophical life and the dialectic.

Then there is the need for the awakening of *ousia* by the power of Love that raises all souls by the desire for Goodness and Beauty.

Last of all, there is the kind of activity that turns about to focus on the source of all and to realize through the turning toward a higher mode of being that they have completed their philosophical journey.

JESUS

Well, I can easily identify Zeus, Poseidon, Athena, Ares, Artemis, Aphrodite, and Apollo, but for the others, I am not sure. Perhaps, with a bit of reflection, I can fill in the list, but you express these in a hierarchical manner and I would like to see that.

SOCRATES

The last ones you probably can recall with a bit of reflection, but I'll set them forward: Zeus, Poseidon, and Hephaestus for the first triad, and for the second, the guardians are Hestia, Athena, and Ares; for the third triad there are Demeter, Hera, and Artemis, while for the last triad there are Hermes, Aphrodite, and Apollo.

Jesus

You are a wonder, Socrates, and pleased I am to see these Gods arranged hierarchically. I do have an interest, as you do, in this last triad. It is a beautiful way to describe the soul's journey. I see now how you use these Gods to present the way of philosophy.

Socrates

They are the intellectual forces that move reason into energy. With this, it joins with the perfection of the soul and body in the soul's quest. This makes possible a true birth of what it has been long seeking.

As the progression of the soul advances, it participates in more intellectual ways and is inspired to ideas that are poetic and profound. Nature needs the proper generation of the soul and body; for without that, nothing further would be possible.

Jesus

It seems that these Gods have a structure that can be represented by this threeness. Do you have a picture in your mind that does represent them all together?

Socrates

Now, you caught me again. Right you are. I do have an image I can share. Picture a triangle whose apex represents Zeus and the right and left lower angles are positions for Poseidon and Hephaestus. Now picture a larger triangle that surrounds and guards that triangle. The apex of the larger triangle is Being, the lower right angle of the larger triangle is for the power and the lower left angle represents activity.

JESUS

There is so much here that I am amazed. What I would like to understand is how you picture this idea of personification. What lies behind this idea of personification, Socrates?

SOCRATES

I am pleased you have chosen the way of going on. The willingness to live most fully and completely one's vision of Truth is to take on the personification of the ideal. The test of that vision is to be willing to be what that vision embodies. For acting out that vision in the most difficult of circumstances is a fire sacrifice for verifying the degree of Truth of that vision. The test forces those who are against that vision to reveal themselves. Those who act this drama out, or portray it for others to see, force all to see what otherwise would remain in the shadows. By taking this path, much falls, but it leaves the field open for a higher vision to unfold.

Among those who understand these personifications, there are some who grasp the meaning more than others. The way Homer or Hesiod refers to the Gods must have made perfect sense to listeners. Some could immediately recognize who speaks best and worst when talking about these Gods. The ability to grasp the meaning of these personifications of the Gods brings with it an intuitive understanding of how to work with metaphors. When these personifications take on a physical form, they become the objects of sculpture and the poetic expression of them is in the oracles and philosophy. By understanding the way these images of the Gods can be related together in drama, we have a natural way of developing analogical thinking.

The task of understanding dreams is nothing else than applying that way of reason to the world of dreams. For, a dream takes an analogical form that contains an anagogic function to raise the souls of man to the divine.

JESUS

I admire the way you are going. To show that dreams can be understood is a new dawn of reason. To be able to show dreams are personally meaningful to those to whom they come is very profound. Who can say man cannot ascend to the Intelligible if dreams disclose their secrets?

SOCRATES

Yes, dreams are the bridge to a most sacred way of understanding. When people seek meaning in dreams, their way of being is enhanced. They awaken a common spirit that brings into being a culture of the Mind.

JESUS

You see the Hellenes are part of that curious breed of dream cultures, and with this cultural awareness they would have had a keen insight into metaphors and similes. I found that very same thing among people I encountered. The culture I was relating to could accept the role of parables as a way of awakening the Mind. There is much in common between dream cultures and cultures that respond to parables, yet there is that difference.

SOCRATES

Indeed, it is because of this background culture that we can say that Prometheus personifies a remarkable foresight that goes beyond mere thinking. His far seeing knows the future as it knows the present. On a personal level, this kind of knowing even knows that it will only do what is providentially the best. On the general level, it is the awareness that a profound structure of Justice is in place because that is what it means to say our Cosmos is providentially Intelligible.

Jesus

Yes, you express it well. However, there are many people who live without a mythology. Even if some of them had it, I wonder if they could bring themselves to understand it. It may be that you Hellenes smile and live without the oppressive hand of punishment and sin upon you all. Surely, the greater the fear, the more the need for a sacrificing punishment. Are you advancing the idea that man is free to enter this Hellenic mind that you have drawn up? But it is dead and over, isn't it?

Socrates

Now, that is a very interesting question. Surely, if ever similar conditions arise, we can expect similar effects. To set in place myths so transparent that they can communicate principles in Nature and of the Mind is truly remarkable. The many years it must have taken to find parallels between such personification and then for people to spell out their relationships with one another is remarkable. The inherent hierarchy among these Gods can add yet another dimension to this utmost craft.

Jesus

You return to the idea of hierarchy, and while there are some things about that idea I am familiar with, there is a question in my mind about the way you use the term. When do you find it important to use the idea of hierarchy?

Socrates

You ask, again, about the idea of hierarchy and that is a good question to reflect upon. Before we explore that idea, let's recall the language of the elements of our theology, because our theology plays a major role in our system. First, then, what ideas are derived from the notion of the One, or the Good? Surely we can say the ideas of oneness, unity, union, communion, wholeness, and the idea of the whole of all wholes are all from that idea. However, if we set aside these ideas that are derived from the One and ask about the One itself, shall we not be surprised to discover it can only be described in negative terms? Again, what if we can describe it in positive terms? Would we not be equally surprised? But, the Good or the One is expressed in negatives, as the Idea of the Good is expressed through positive terms. Here is the difference between the Good and the Idea of the Good. Again, what if this second term, the Idea of the Good, can be experienced in all its fullness as perfect, as pure Beauty, as ultimate Reality, always the same as an unchanging eternal most luminous light of Being, and that it brings with it an insight into the meaning of existence? Is it possible that the next term might be something that when taken as a whole has many parts, passes in and out of existence, and is never at rest? Then, these three ideas seem to be linked together in a descending manner and if each can be said to be either the cause or the condition for the next, then what would you say we have?

Jesus

I see what you are doing. You are presenting a metaphysical view of creation as it proceeds from the One, to Being (which is ultimate Reality), then to Soul. They stand as a basic triad, so you call those terms being arranged in a hierarchy, do you not?

Socrates

Yes, indeed. Now, take the idea of the God of theism; what ideas follow from this idea, as our set of terms for the One followed from it?

JESUS

Well, they don't have a parallel set of terms; that is clear.

SOCRATES

Then again, if some kind of reasoning can express the kinship these terms have, then is it possible that the same kind of reasoning can be applied to more fundamental ideas?

JESUS

I do like what you are saying. Now, in what way might it proceed from the highest term to the lower?

SOCRATES

If we reason about it further and attempt to describe how these ideas can be said to relate to one another, we can say that in this hierarchical arrangement of terms, each generates an image of itself and in the process imitates its own birth, bringing a likeness akin to itself into being. Equally, what is prior to each in the hierarchy subsumes within itself the majesty and power revealed in its subsequent, or we can say the relation of the antecedent to its consequent is that of model to copy, or object and its shadow. In generating each, the process repeats itself within each level, so that as each is a center that generates circles, it reflects the power and intelligence in a particular way.

JESUS

Then I assume you assign Gods to these hierarchical principles and create your mythology. Is that correct?

SOCRATES

Yes, that is so, and then it is possible to allegorize these so-called myths to show parallels with the spiritual plane.

Jesus

The language of Hellenic myths falls on deaf ears in the lands of Judea.

Socrates

Yes, to allegorize myths means you learn a new way of reasoning. It challenges the mind to find forces in Nature and among mankind that can be summarized into images and forms consistent with and representative of higher forces. It does another thing of importance: it holds back those who would take the myths literally. A people without a mythology we call barbarians, or strangers to the Gods.

Jesus

True it is. I have often heard how you Greeks call many people barbarians. Your people have borrowed from many countries and polished them with principles and created through them all the arts. Much of your profound thought seems to have been drawn from Egypt, and that makes us akin in that regard. Remarkable it is. You do see the task of you Greeks to bring others into your way of being and reasoning, don't you? Truly, it is a formidable task you set for yourselves.

Socrates

What lies behind bringing man from a barbarian existence, living a brutal and short life, to the flowering of a culture of excellence? Is there a need to explain this transformation? Greek mythology offers a way to gain insight into the problem. It can be said that mythology is the collective dream of a people. The same way of understanding the one follows for the other. Consider: one of these Gods of the Hellenes recognized the promise in man and stole the arts and fire from Heaven to turn man around, and doing so, to come to know himself. He saved man and suffered for his theft. There is no original sin here, no Garden of Eden with its account of how evil trumps good. Here we have a victory and kinship between man and the Gods.

Let us turn to sacrifice. Prometheus taught man how to sacrifice: When sacrificing, always separate what is not essential to one's life into one pile and into another what sustains and provides for one's health and growth. Disguise the one to appear as the other. Offer what does not benefit you to the Gods and call your friends together for a banquet of food and words from the other. What you don't need and does not benefit, you offer to the God. Or we could say, Do not do what you hate, but sacrifice your hate to the Gods. Striving for excellence in the arts means to be willing to sacrifice what blocks one from attaining it. Sacrifice your problems to the Gods. Those who participate in this Hellenic culture naturally gain a way of thinking and being that separates them from all others. The quest for excellence is open to all. Those with a kinship and ability to master an art gain access to a different way of being. Becoming a Hellene is open to male and female. So here are a people sprung as it were from the actions and duty of a God, a far-seeking God who sacrifices for man's growth and nurture. The arts, fire, and dialectic Prometheus stole from Zeus and gave them to man as gifts. In that gift he sanctified the arts. It is through them that the people of the Earth can sustain themselves, can reach the Intelligible, and come to wonder about its source.

If the idea of sacrifice means the willingness to sacrifice what one most treasures and loves, and to be willing to join forces with a destructive fury that ends all life, then we must ask: If a God is so separated from Justice can he be a God at all? The God of Abraham serves the purpose of bringing unity to a people at a price of waging wars on earth that culminate in the final destruction of all life. Shall we say all this is because a jealous God needs to conquer his adversary, Satan? From this, we can see why they are forbidden to create an image of their God and cannot be allowed to even think they can comprehend their God. It is likely that to view that image and to reflect on the nature of such a God would challenge the continued existence of their faith.

Jesus

We should remember that one of our differences is that with your reason you can always start off with a clean slate. With those like me, we must assume the traditions of our fathers and then try to change the literal to the spiritual level of meaning. So, with reason you can easily start your dialectic with the rejection of our Abrahamic God, but we cannot. Well, Socrates, we have gone along this path of the dialectic, and now what other distinctions shall you make?

Socrates

Among those who follow a tribal God, there are those who we can call descendants of Abraham. While there are now several distinct groups, their differences override their similarities. The animosity of these groups with one another spawns countless wars and acts of violence directed at each other. As a whole, these religions unite against those who reject their message. The core belief of sacrifice they share betrays their own fundamental weakness.

Jesus

To continue your thought, I would add something to pull together what we have said about this movement that it has been said I started. First, if those who call themselves Christian do so because they accept Paul's vision of Jesus, they do gain some support from the last gospel of the New Testament, the Gospel of John. So these must be called Pauline-John followers.

Socrates

I follow along with what you are saying, and for my part I would say something about what we are calling the Hellenes. They are the ones who recognize that mindfulness is not a matter of birth, race, or anything other than acknowledging that the dignity of man comes from the freedom to express the Mind. I have found the most dramatic presentation of this theme in that great play of Aeschylus, *Suppliant Maidens*. Among these Hellenes, there are those who go on to gain fundamental insights into the nature of Mind. Again, of these, some go on to experience the majesty and the beauty of the luminous light of Being. However, as much as these two groups vary, they are drawn to seek to understand such profound experiences. As a group, most seek to enter these states of Mind through the Eleusinian mysteries, but the mark of the Hellenic is to seek excellence in an understanding of all that is. That is the very thing they seek to achieve in the arts, mathematics, astronomy, biology, and architecture.

Jesus

You sharpen the difference between these two very clearly. The Abrahamic religions are truly closed belief systems! They do not continue from any prior tradition, they spring from primary figures, and from them, they contain the whole.

Socrates

I have come to see that the Abrahamic religions share much with the Zoroastrians, while they ignore the sameness. There is much that can be said about these religions as being closed.

Jesus

How do you understand what I have said?

Socrates

If I express it I will need to contrast it with the Hellenic tradition.

Jesus

I would be delighted to hear it.

Socrates

In those closed systems no further development can occur within them unless they break away and form a sub-group. They have no connection to any past, and no connection with anything in their future. They have the moment that is isolated and out of history. Within themselves, they cannot admit change without collapsing. Now, consider the difference. The future is open to the Hellenes. I'll show you what I see for them. I will put it in general terms and you for your part will furnish the names.

The understanding of the Hellenic Gods as a harmony of certain ideas attributed to each of these Gods would be easily recognized by the Hellenes. The differences in the tales of the Gods would be subjects of discussion that would reveal the level of understanding of a spokesman. Each personification and tale of the Gods would be like strands woven into the tapestry of Wisdom.

The shallow understanding of these images and tales would clearly be recognized as something discordant. The ability to understand these ideas within their particular drama, or myth, gives a natural affinity with dream analysis. Such people would generate a dream culture. The inability to grasp the meanings behind the image would clearly mark those who can only function on a literal and concrete level of mind. A keen nurturing of the tales of the Gods, or mythology, is the way of using the Mind to know the Mind as participating in the works of the Mind.

Chorus

So we are here listening to an appeal for a return of the Gods of Ancient Greece. You sure don't need an argument against that idea.

We left those pagan ideas and burnt down their temples and wiped 'em out because nothing good can follow from worshipping many Gods. How would anyone know which one you should pray to? Go ahead and tell me and I'll tell you that all you've got is a bunch of pipe dreams that you call reasoning. No one can describe what is really going on and that's all you need to know.

Anti-Chorus

You are listening without hearing the reasons for what you reject and that's all you can do. Try it for once and see if you can at least listen to what is going on. Perhaps you should ask yourself: What is the source of your anger? Why do you scream aloud? Is it to silence your own doubts and fears?

Jesus

Socrates, I do believe we should explore those ideas that separate us. Unless we review them we will not have gained much. Certainly, sin and error, good and evil, wisdom and ignorance need to be reviewed.

Socrates

Our differences should not be brushed off.

Jesus

Let me ask you to start off.

Socrates

Good enough, I would ask this: Is what is called evil, or bad acts, the consequence of not being able to do the good that should be done?

Jesus

Yes, and to add to that some believe there is even a punishment for an ignorance that cannot be overcome with learning. We call that the sin against the Holy Ghost, since even though you don't know if you blasphemed against the Holy Ghost, eternal punishment is your lot.

SOCRATES

Would you say then, for these believers, that there is a kind of ignorance that is more powerful and pervasive than any wisdom? Or, would you counter that there is no ignorance that can stand the light of Wisdom and survive?

JESUS

Wisdom and ignorance cannot exist together.

SOCRATES

Would you go along with me and say that it would be foolish to punish for a lack of Wisdom if there is a Wisdom that can overcome ignorance?

JESUS

Your questions carry along the weight of what was said before. I would have to say that from what we have said, Socrates, that for the wise it is possible to live without sin.

SOCRATES

Interesting that along with its fall, so goes the value of punishment. Could there be a wrongdoer who didn't know that what he did was wrong? Surely, it would be worth a bit of effort to explore why we do not look at mistakes to see why they occurred, instead of punishing for making mistakes. So a failure to learn makes mistakes possible—curious.

JESUS

I, too, find that something to puzzle over.

SOCRATES

Do those who suffer painful punishment gain Wisdom or do they learn the cost they must pay for being caught?

JESUS

Yes, that is the crime of punishment!

SOCRATES

Then no one should be punished for a failure to learn, but rather should be shown its dreadful consequences.

JESUS

I say yes to that.

SOCRATES

The word *sin* is not Greek, and it carries with it many negative associations. However, in Greek the word for *sin* is *amartion* and simply means "missing the mark," as an archer would say if his arrow missed the target. What follows? Well, the idea of *amartion*, or "missing the mark," is an error, so there is no issue here.

JESUS

That is true.

SOCRATES

There cannot be a clash between good and evil if the Good Is. If evil cannot know the Good without losing its existence, and if it lacks Wisdom in its acts, then it cannot be an opponent in the true sense.

JESUS

True it is.

SOCRATES

Do not the evildoers believe they are justified in their acts? However, if Justice is always accompanied with Wisdom, then no evil act can be seen as an act of justice because it lacks Wisdom.

JESUS

I do like your questions, and it speaks well for those discussions you have engaged in, Socrates.

SOCRATES

In those discussions, we went even further. We asked if there is a wisdom that can overcome evil, for if there is, it would be foolish to punish for a lack of wisdom. Because the effects of punishment always bring a particular kind of suffering that dominates the soul, it deprives one of the freedom to discover the roots of one's folly. Beyond that, it leaves untouched the core beliefs that are fundamental to man's ignorance.

JESUS

So, puzzling along our way, we can say if there is no justice in punishment then there would be no need for Hell or Hades. However, this forces the astonishing conclusion that there is no need for a God that allows or plays a role in punishment.

SOCRATES

Yes, it brings to the foreground the question of the nature of the deity we call God. The kind of God we are building together is one that knows the Mind of man. Because learning plays a vital role in this drama we are part of, we can say it moves with the spirit of Justice and Wisdom, can we not?

JESUS

Well, it looks like you know how to use those Promethean gifts. However, my dear Socrates, should we not consider this: If the Cosmos has no place for punishment, then that means those who do wrong can escape the consequences of their doing wrong. What joy those who have committed the worst of crimes must experience if they learn that no punishment awaits them! Then there will be no after-death experiences of a Hell in the House of Hades!

SOCRATES

While there may not be an after-world of punishment, there is a place where what is deserved plays out its hand with precision and skill. Where? Right here in the Cosmos. For this world, this everyday world, with all its sufferings and confusions, is the result of people in the present living out the influences of all that they have learned and cultivated in their present and from their former reincarnations. Whatever the soul has done to others will be done to them. The deed and its consequence are perfectly balanced. In this way, there is a just rendering of deeds and their consequences. However, pure Justice shows itself when the soul reverts upon itself to surface and eliminate those blocks to the soul's excellence.

The soul survives death and is reincarnated, carrying along with it whatever it has learned and nurtured from its past. Justice plays out its hand, assuring that each soul receives its most proper due. Look at the extreme suffering many souls experience in each of the days on Earth and you'll see the past playing out its justice on Earth.

JESUS

I am carried away by your way of reasoning. However, it is well known that your Odysseus gained entry into Hades and saw the souls of many brave warriors and those of noble women enduring suffering for their sins. From what we have said, shall we say Homer is not among the sages?

SOCRATES

Those who come to realize the Self feast and banquet here in our heavens, while those in Hades carry the burden of their masks and receive their punishment for the fraud they committed, on the one hand, and, on the other, they gain the rewards from whatever good they achieved until the power of their actions is dissipated. So it was said of Hercules, the Hellenics favorite hero.

JESUS

Yes, that follows with our way of going. For Justice to reign, there must be rewards for honoring and knowing the Self. I agree that man needs to see and understand that through learning every sin loses its sustaining power over man. I would add that beyond these things, man must learn why ignorance has the power it has. For surely, that is what you would say, is it not, Socrates?

SOCRATES

Sure thing. If our earthly existence is where we can learn the roots of our unsuspected false beliefs about ourselves, then it is also where we can turn towards the quest for the Wisdom of the Self.

JESUS

Why would you say that it is in man's earthly existence that we can gain these jewels?

SOCRATES

There can only be one answer, because the conditions necessary for learning are present when a soul is in the body. For the kind of learning we are exploring, having a body is a necessity. You need a body to learn. To experience a puzzle that is unsolved yet real is to feel perplexed. To feel numbed by realizing you do not know what you thought you knew is a shock the body feels. To experience a feeling of joy at coming to a conclusion needs a body to experience its impact.

The willingness to go along in the search for an answer is to be awakened to the need for an experience of knowing. This stage of learning does not need to add something, because it experiences through the body a dropping away of the pretense of knowing. There is no need to have to remember it. At this point, there is nothing there to remember. However, being in an open state one can follow a lead to discover an answer. Going back over this process again and again is to always be open to a deeper learning.

Jesus

Your advice to them would be to sing goodbye to repentance, retribution, and salvation. You would strip them of what had guided them in their life. I wonder if the difference lies in facing the finality of this life and death in comparison with your belief in reincarnation.

Socrates

If Justice plays a decisive role, then there must be reincarnation. What other than this idea can make sense of the vast injustice we see everywhere?

Jesus

From what you have said, I would say you believe the justification of this principle lies entirely in your idea that man is in a cycle of reincarnation because he is here to learn. Would you say that what man must learn is to end the cycle of all clan beliefs and go on to know himself?

What if before the next reincarnation the soul might say, "no more, thanks, I'd rather not be incarnated." To whatever degree the soul is aware that it is facing a life where misery and suffering is its lot, why not pull back and say "no"?

SOCRATES

We are a race that is here to fulfill its destiny. The end is everywhere present. To come to Know Thyself is to realize the nature of Reality is divine. Our task is complicated because we seek other goals and have other loyalties. We are here to master our present fate and seek to fulfill our destiny. The kind of problems we return to again and again are loyalties to other than our sacred goal. The loyalty to other than that goal is the nature of our problems.

We have talked about the kind of problems the race of man experiences as they identify with the values of the family clan. Recall that one of the mysteries we have discussed is why the child believes something about himself that is false. What is it in the transmission of the core beliefs of the family that makes believable what is false? However, is it not true that in accepting this core belief, it creates a way of being and an identity? This identity plays a decisive role in our choice of our next incarnation.

JESUS

So, as the child accepts a new way of being that marks and shapes his way of life, so in reincarnation, the soul accepts a way of life that marks and shapes his or her new life. You have laid out the mystery in a splendid way, Socrates. There must be something similar in both to account for the identification with or the loyalty to their new image and way of life.

SOCRATES

The similarity that you ask about is the dynamic mean between our twofold existence. As we journey between Heaven and Earth, this bond that is experienced accounts for the full range of the self-imposed masks that block the perception of the Self.

Consider, as we know, upon death all experience that most brilliant light of Being. To the degree one is able to endure that divine luminosity, to that very degree there is a corresponding profound depth or shallowness of one's way of being. In that encounter they realize that what blocked them from a more profound experience was their own fear that they would be extinguished in that awesome and powerful presence of luminosity.

JESUS

Does the role of similarity play itself out as the pathologos is transmitted? If so, when does it happen?

SOCRATES

There is always a time when the child steps out of the generally accepted state of mind that marks the family psyche. It seems natural, beautiful, and has a sense of freedom to it. At this moment, the parental figure has to end that freedom or the clan will have to deal with a freedom of expression in other ways that are unsettling to the family ways of being. Whatever the incident is, it becomes the object of scorn and condemnation; that way of being becomes taboo, and when that happens, the state of mind that accompanies the way of being is linked and also forbidden. To make the false appear true the parental figure has to appear most noble, as knowing the truth about life, as being the utmost sincere and caring. These scenes are always rare, and the child sees what it is to be knowing and caring, and this becomes the way of being to imitate. It creates a new way of being, which is a new way of life for the child. With this new vision the child gladly accepts the clan-belief that gives the appearance of excellence. It is a pseudo-excellence.

We find the same thing going on as flocks of people go to see excellence unfold in front of them. They admire the excellence they see. It inspires them to achieve something similar in their own lives.

Jesus

The drive for excellence is the fuel for an inner life. It shapes them and they become more real in themselves. How did you describe to your people the end of all this seeking?

Socrates

When death arrives, all who are capable of this kind of learning take what has been learned and what has nurtured them into their next life. Whatever is yet to be learned and realized becomes what must be returned to in another life. Man as a whole is part of this struggle to "Know Thyself." It is a cosmic dance of meaning that ends when there is nothing left to learn, and the race of man ends in the state no longer of man but that to which he has joined himself.

Jesus

Well said, well said, Socrates. I appreciate those words and they must have come from no other source than the Logos.

Socrates

Yes, the Logos drives the chariot of our soul and leads us to those mighty doors of Justice that offer a passageway to the eternal.

Jesus

There is good reason why you were called a sage, Socrates. Yet, from what I have heard, there is some confusion about whether or not you truly know. If so, you are admitting to an ignorance of the worst kind. How can your soul soar aloft if you are among the ignorant? Shall I say that among the sages you were the only one who said that you weren't a sage? You did say, from what I heard, that you know nothing of what is beautiful or good, yet you were included among that group of sages, were you not?

SOCRATES

We have both heard the same thing and there is very little truth in it. It is an old problem. If you want to make some teaching private so it can earn the title of being esoteric, all you have to do is to state it clearly and simply and you will find no one will get it.

JESUS

Now, that is something new to me. Please make it clear for me. Surely, it is something I am going to benefit from.

SOCRATES

What I did conclude was "what I do not know, I do not think I do."

JESUS

You present a simple saying here without ambiguity, so where was the confusion?

SOCRATES

Many have taken that saying of mine and understood it as saying that I do not know. They toast that saying as if I said that I am truly ignorant, but of what? The state of the Self as One is beyond names and the Logos, so it is beyond knowing. How do you understand my saying, Jesus?

JESUS

From what you have said, it means that you can never make a mistake about what you do know.

Socrates

Yes, or you could say that once one gains what we call pure Knowledge, it is impossible to mistake it for anything else. Its paramount uniqueness must be staggeringly different from all else. Hence, it is impossible to mistake it for anything else.

Jesus

And, to know that is Wisdom, most interesting that is. Let me ask you another question, Socrates, since the many out there thought you were wrong, and they prosecuted you. They saw you as very wrong about your beliefs. They saw you as a lawbreaker, and you stood trial; you were sentenced and executed. Certainly, you experienced punishment, but can you say it was just? I ask that because with you, it seems we can see the necessity for a just punishment. So, that punishment is justified, at least here.

Socrates

Yes, it is good to review my defense. Let's review it and see what we can see. First, I was guilty of not believing in the Gods of the State, but of introducing new spiritual things instead. My defense was to show that it was true; I admitted a voice comes to me and guides me through my life. I even admitted that something spiritual and divine often comes to me. Truly, I said to my jurors that I have been commanded by God through oracles, dreams, and in every way any word of God comes to man to be a philosopher.

Jesus

Being a philosopher as you are is being a divine being. How was that received?

Socrates

The people of Athens did not have a clear picture of what a philosopher was and the practices of a philosopher. It seemed to them that I was strange and strange I was. In not knowing that a philosopher was sent to them for their true benefit, they were confused.

Jesus

And, rightly so. This unknowing became a prejudice against you and against all those who must have been seen to be like you.

Socrates

What was remarkable is that the city of Athens gave me a chance to confront that prejudice against all philosophers. I could be my own spokesman. It was through my trial that I could dialogue with the whole of Athens. There are few cities that would allow a man to defend himself and challenge the law itself that he was charged with breaking.

Jesus

True that is, Socrates. It was a rare and beautiful thing that Athens allowed.

Socrates

Yes, just consider what a gift it was. The legal system of Athens gave me a chance to confront and remove the prejudice that the many in the jury had about what a philosopher is. I was allowed to challenge my accusers directly. In such an unusual setting, I was allowed to present my vision and practice of philosophy. I told them I was sent by God to awaken the sleeping souls of man by stinging them with questions about the nature of man and the divine. I explained it was through dreams and oracles that I received guidance.

Jesus

It is true that dreams are a way to receive messages, but those in my tradition have scarcely touched on this way of approaching the divine. Apart from your busy dream life, how was your way of practicing philosophy received?

Socrates

As for this philosophical practice of mine, I told them there is nothing more significant than my being the gadfly awakening man from his sleep of normalcy. Sure it is that I am the rare gift from God. If a society allows unjust laws to be challenged, then it has just laws. Putting on the stage of public view the prejudices of the many makes visible their folly. It sacrifices the wise to preserve the beliefs of society. In a just society, the just way of life of philosophers challenges the unjust laws and prejudices of their fellow man.

Jesus

My judgment is like others who have learned of your trial. Clearly, you gave evidence against yourself because your judgment was to defend Truth against the prejudices of society. You are judged guilty as charged while being innocent. The charges were just and your defense was just. Your place is among the philosophical heroes. I am equally guilty of doing something similar, but not analogous to your Prometheus. I urge those who are bound by tribal Gods to escape from those fetters. For that God who personifies the quest to Know Thyself knows that to return to that source is the true goal of all Intelligible life.

Socrates

The trial was fair, the judgment too was fair, and the punishment was fair. I was guilty of the charges of introducing new spiritual things into Athenian society. If they had freed me, they would have had to change the law from that day forward.

JESUS

Can what follows the punishment that society pours upon their fellow man bring about a good? The society that punishes has its own history, and as each society defends their primary beliefs, so they create their laws. As a result, they are doing the legal thing, but they have not reached for what was just. Athens, you say, was rare, but if so, what do you find special about the history of Athens?

SOCRATES

Athens was a rare historical event. It was the expression of vast and profound forces coming together, and because of this it is not likely to be repeated in history. A society like Athens gave its citizens the freedom to break an unjust law and then to subject it to the voice of reason. The legitimacy of the law itself is put into question. The trial forces a review of the justice of the law and the punishment. The court reviews the rationality behind law as it applies to the best of its citizens and those feared to be the worst. I was allowed an opportunity to dialogue with my accusers and present my case before 501 in the jury. Punishment? I did not suffer, it caused me no anguish, and I smiled my way through the doorway of death. Was anything learned? Yes, the people of Athens learned the price they paid for upholding an unjust law.

JESUS

Truly, there are cities that stand as symbols for mankind to contemplate and among them Athens and Jerusalem shine with a particular brightness. What gave them that sacred mark reaches into strange hypotheses about the future of mankind. Your reincarnation brought you into a most brilliant stage of history. Through this event, you arrived at the stage in history for your destiny to be known to all of mankind.

Socrates

Yes, the glory of Athens is unique. Destiny and the future of mankind shake hands. When society turns towards Mind and the things of Mind, there is the flowering of culture, but when it turns criminal and becomes oppressive, my kind of philosophy cannot play its public role.

Jesus

Well done, but now these are the words of Plato, are they not? So what is it he missed?

Socrates

If he were able to know such things, Plato should have shared with us what dreams and oracles shaped his destiny. Notice Plato's statement of my claim that what has come to me includes "in every way in which some divine influence has ever come to man." Clearly, this is worth explaining. The claim is as startling to hear as it is to accept. I claimed that any way in which anyone in the past has ever been influenced by the divine has also happened to me. There are not many claims that can match that one.

Jesus

I wonder about this issue that is in front of us. You think that it is best for the wise among us to talk openly about what has shaped their spiritual life. That, of course, means no secret doctrine needs to be shared only with a few chosen ones. If you are right, then there is no need for an esoteric tradition.

Chorus

It is always the same. Just get a clever speaker and let 'em address the crowd, and he'll pull everything down. This dialogue stuff is foolish. In each exchange, if you don't agree completely you are dragged along to a conclusion you don't like. Look at this, no punishment. Look at the new solution and laugh. Instead of Hell, you get reborn here on Earth. So you get away with as much as you can. Who wouldn't want to be reborn here rather than the terrible hellish punishments man faces in the after world? Next, just pick your own idea of God. Go ahead. Get one that is nice and simple. Get one that can't punish for disobeying and you'll find no God at all. You don't pick a God to make your philosophy smile. You are stuck with the one you have been taught and that's all you need.

Now we see the whole of it. Get this straight. Mankind doesn't need anything new or even a rebuilt truth. What we have is enough. Even if you reject belief and faith, that is better than making believe in reason and understanding. You can't save yourself with the crazy thinking you call understanding. It is mad to think you can understand Reality and God. Dump it quick.

Madness is where we are, and you can see it being spelled out all around. Philosophy was killed; there is nothing in it. No one gives a damn about it. You can't wake up what was a fierce ghost. It is better to fill your mind with junk than these absurdities. I'll scream out a truth you ought to hear. You people who assume you know, all you intellectuals, are the problem. Get rid of them. We are the only real people. We are the ones because that's all you need. Don't fill our kids with empty and impossible dreams. Life is too damn difficult just by itself. If you add more of this stuff, you'll be digging your own grave. Yes, we are in a war against you guys who blow your own horn. Intellectuals are all pussyfooted idiots who drive us all mad. I'll tell you the truth, if you care to hear it. All the wars since the beginning of our mass movements have all been against you guys. Fascism, Nazism, Communism, they are all against your kind. It has always been a war against you guys. Right now, it takes many forms, but it is right here. All you want is to help those who can't bear to help themselves. There are too many of us on this planet, so wiping out you guys will end more than one problem. You want to get rid of core beliefs? Well, I will tell you that these core beliefs are what are trusted. We finally have a religion of the people that people can believe in, so why don't you just shut up if you can't get into believing?

ANTI-CHORUS

Your voices speak the truth, wonderful it is. Yes, Socrates surely is a clever speaker. For all your yelling aloud why don't you put on the table your best example of punishment? Open up your example and show how the punishment benefits the wrongdoer. Point out how the punishment keeps the wrongdoer from doing his misdeeds again and again. Show how the wrongdoer learned something that benefitted them other than to try to avoid being caught for wrongdoing. Yes, you have to pick a God; you need to review carefully what you see necessary if this Cosmos has been brought into existence from higher Intelligible causes.

The idea of God or Theology one has should be drawn with care. It should encompass all that reflects the ideas of Perfection, Truth, Goodness, Beauty, and then see why the most profound of superlatives can be assigned to that divine luminosity. But these most fundamental ideas are denied of the One or the Good itself. Take a look at what's being said. Are you afraid to? Don't worry about seeing that your basic ideas are hollow and empty of meaning; you'll still believe what has convinced you was true.

JESUS

Interesting it is, Socrates, how we moved from punishment to the idea of reincarnation.

SOCRATES

Yes, the after-death experience that all will encounter is the luminous light of divine Being: overwhelming in its profound

Beauty, Real beyond anything else, and seeing directly that this is not different from pure Mind itself. Radiating Goodness, it brings an awe-inspiring presence to all.

JESUS

Inspired by that majesty, they seek to find it in themselves and in what they do. So this becomes the source of the urge to try again with another birth to catch that golden ring. You have done it, Socrates, you have made the point that we live in a parallel Cosmos that links the dynamics of both Heaven and Earth with a spirit of Justice and Truth.

I do like that you have shown that it is just that each soul has its unique problems. To escape those problems, Justice is always present as an inner guide. Problems for the soul are gifts for our growth. To try to escape from those problems is itself the problem.

SOCRATES

So we can say that there are always necessary conditions for each problem to exist, as there is its solution. What's that but that the pathologos is a rational structure that has its own logic, but it proceeds from a faulty core belief? The pathologos cannot stand in the light of the Logos, can it?

JESUS

Socrates, what ideas do you say constitute these core primal beliefs? I ask because they are likely to be different from what I take them to be. I would like to see how you express them.

SOCRATES

There are several core beliefs and the idea of God is primary. It is linked to the idea of Justice. If there isn't a major and fundamental place for Justice within a system, there is chaos. While good and bad behavior may indeed have their consequences after death, they need to be balanced with an obvious way of learning, which is to know how to avoid the one and gain the other. Where? Well, mankind is born to learn and to fulfill his destiny; learning what is good as well as the highest Good is primary. Punishment and rewards follow mankind in the afterworld, or the House of Hades. However, only an earthly form of learning can provide the rich insights into Justice. Justice needs to be known in the particular and acted upon. It is from these early learning events that the soul comes to the idea of Justice. Once these ideas are unified, the soul of each has a justification for its way of being and it defines its relations with their fellow man.

JESUS

I have heard that you say that taking on a human form is the very condition for learning. Yes, the soul is what learns, but its need for the body is not fully understood, is it?

SOCRATES

What is man? A union of the body and the soul makes possible learning because in learning, the form of the thing learned becomes transparently one's own. All learning, be it music, mathematics, or language, once truly learned, can bring the soul to act without recalling what was learned. Once learned, it is possible to act spontaneously through the object learned, and that state of excellence is an experience of the Mind itself. It is an openness, a wonderful freedom to act without thinking, yet that state of freedom makes possible acts that are totally appropriate to one's circumstances. Much of human learning is by rote, but it does not achieve this inner state of mind and that surely is a loss if that is all that is offered. It is this union of the body and the soul into what is a complete being that makes the human being. It is no different from the informing principle which brings to a unity the different parts and organs of the body into a single being. The turning about to discover what learning is, and its furthermost reach, raises that union to a spiritual union that marks the pursuit of philosophy.

JESUS

You said that you met with a group of sages after your death and it is likely they discussed these very ideas. Hesiod and Homer were among them. Your own views must have brought the discussions into sharp focus, so how did the talks go and what idea did you center on? I have had a deep interest in this because it is well known here that your Plato has said that the philosophy Diotima initiated you into rivals the divinely inspired Hesiod and Homer. Share with me then how the talks went.

SOCRATES

Yes, a fine group they were. There was Orpheus, whose music gave him power even over the House of Hades. He added much to our talks, and so did his son, Musaios, the most profound of seers and the prophet who declared that Justice was the daughter of Zeus. When Homer and Hesiod joined us, we were able to join our voices in a choir of song in praise of Truth and Wisdom.

JESUS

Do share with me the divinely inspired reflections your group engaged in.

SOCRATES

We often returned to these core beliefs that most often block access to that unity of ideas. The two principal ideas were that there is a ruling God, or divinity, of the afterworld, and it is this God who passes judgment over the souls of the dead and assigns rewards and punishments. Our discussions turned on this question: What idea of God is consistent with the nature of punishment and what is not?

Jesus

From what we have said, it seems there is only one conclusion. I am cautious about coming to it, even though my mind has already announced its presence.

Socrates

These two are the most essential and fundamental ideas that are linked to other ideas, forming a closed system of ideas that brings to birth the ideal of Justice.

Jesus

Then take me along that discussion on punishment, and then tell me about what you have come to about the nature of God.

Socrates

Good idea, there, Jesus. We will have to take a few steps that Musaios took me through. I'll frame the questions just as he did, and you, in turn, answer them, as you like. However, I should say that when I entered the talks, I started in my usual way that I can easily review. I started by asking if we could explore what differences there are between making mistakes, doing something incorrectly, being wrong about something, and sin.

Jesus

Now, I like that way of going. I'd say we are off to a good beginning.

SOCRATES

I started with a few simple questions: "Is it true that to help someone who made mistakes in Geometry that you would first have to understand it yourself?" Then I asked, "Before offering some teaching to overcome the error, would you first need to grasp what kind of mistake or error was being made? Did the student make a mistake because he was evil or because he failed to apply some principle? Or is your idea of evil restricted to moral problems and if so, it lacks a general scope."

JESUS

No, not punishment, only teaching would help overcome such mistakes and errors.

SOCRATES

If mistakes and errors are correctable by gaining a better understanding or knowledge of the subject, then does sin fall in this class of correctable things?

JESUS

Interesting question you have here. You are asking if the failure of understanding gives birth to sin.

SOCRATES

Yes, does the failure of understanding of what is right and lawful bring about the need for instruction or for punishment?

JESUS

In my youth, I heard it drummed into my ears that punishment should follow when learning fails. When one knows better and does the worse, there is a failure of will and learning. For all the screaming aloud of this refrain, I always have seen in each person's sin a flaw that is correctable by listening to the voice of the divine. Please continue.

Socrates

We have heard similar things. In our discussion, a turn in our talk occurred when Orpheus stressed that to view punishment in the extreme, we need to enter that dreadful House of Hades. While we were reflecting on his remark, Musaios urged that before all else, we must consider the demands of Justice, since it alone will force upon us the need to seek the Truth we so sorely need to see.

Jesus

What are the demands of Justice, Socrates? I haven't heard that phrase used before.

Socrates

Musaios urged us to recognize that with our way of reasoning, we just might be able to bring to light some answers to these questions, but it would be seeing it only in general terms and not in particulars. He said if you want to really discuss the idea of Justice, then you should find a perfect example of the acts of a just man and of an unjust man. An idea should include its opposite, Musaios said. Equally, he said that to balance the discussion, it is necessary to find a woman who stands above all others as a model for an ideal woman, just as the just man should be a model for the ideal man.

Jesus

I like those distinctions. Did the other sages add to it? I would have expected Homer or Hesiod would have something to say.

SOCRATES

It was after Musaios' remarks that Homer smiled and said, "I have just what you want. In my *Iliad* I have the worst of men, Achilles, and in my *Odyssey*, the best of women, Penelope. Look no further." With Achilles, we have the worst of men turning around and becoming the hero of the age. In one man, Achilles, we have the worst becoming the best. With woman, we learn that the Gods sing praises not of Achilles or Odysseus, but for Penelope. Homer offered a prize if we could answer why the greatest hero, Heracles, could be, at the same time, both in the House of Hades and feasting in heaven with the Gods.

JESUS

Again, I find this way of proceeding very interesting. You asked if the most wicked of men, one totally steeped in an arrogance that far exceeds that of all men, could turn around and discover the roots of his folly and become an ideal for all mankind. Then you are asking if there is a woman so free of sin that she can become a perfect model for all women to come. Through these, you want to see how reward and punishment play out in Hades.

SOCRATES

The sage Homer, the most illustrious of poets, sang the song that answered our questions.

JESUS

I see that in my joyous contemplation I missed those wondrous talks. Did Homer identify the worst man in the House of Hades so that we could learn more about man's fate? What did it reveal?

SOCRATES

First, we asked if it is true that punishment always follows a failure of learning. Is what is called evil, or bad acts, the consequence of not knowing what should have been done? Is there a punishment for an ignorance that cannot be overcome with learning? For if so, there is some ignorance more powerful and pervasive than any wisdom. Or is there no ignorance that can stand the light of Wisdom and survive?

Jesus

I do like your questions and it speaks well for those heavenly discussions you have engaged in, Socrates.

Socrates

In those discussions, we did go further. We asked if there is a wisdom that can overcome evil, for then it would be foolish to punish for a lack of Wisdom. Since the effects of punishment always bring a particular kind of suffering that dominates the soul, it deprives one of the freedom to discover the roots of their folly.

Jesus

Now I find that very interesting. Surely, all of those you mentioned must have known that there is the House of Hades. I would like to hear more about how those discussions went.

Socrates

Those discussions dealing with the issue of punishment did come to an end. We went on to delve more deeply into the nature of God.

Jesus

What's that? Did not your Homer fill Hades with lost souls undergoing no end of punishment? Surely, of all interpreters of these things, he must be counted on as one harboring these core primal ideas of punishment.

SOCRATES

We start where we left off, and having had a glimpse of shining Reality, one descends to experience the consequences of identifying with the thoughts, images, and experiences that marked one's former existence. What if what is passed on in the next reincarnation is only what one has learned and nurtured? If that is all, then tell me what happens to all the mistakes, or what you call sins that each soul carries along with it. Could the power of those deeds carry on until they are dissipated? For if so, the consequences and sufferings, and rewards for the good deeds are carried into the next world where what we call the shades play out their existence in the House of Hades.

JESUS

You are very insightful and have delved deeply into these arcane matters. There is much that you have said that is new to me just as what I have said must be new to you. I find what you have said simple and direct, yet for all that I am still puzzled about what you can see as Achilles' fatal flaw. From what we have covered, it must be a core belief about God intertwined with Achilles' own personal pathologos, which I understand to be a false belief about himself. So each soul brings along with it the conditions for its own hell. Then, there just might be some truth in the idea that there is no hell, just its illusion, which is created by each soul as it passes on to its next reincarnation. What now for Achilles?

SOCRATES

It is one thing to believe you have a very special relation to your God and another thing to know the will of that God and how it unfolds in your life. Achilles believed that he was not only favored by Zeus, but that Justice would vindicate whatever his plans were. The action he planned was to gain a final revenge for Agamemnon's captivity of his wife. He sent Patroclus into combat disguised as him, and he plotted to collect his reward for the deception, to have his wife returned to him from her captivity and sail away with his legions. He knew Hector would break off combat and allow him to flee unharmed. Without Achilles defending the ships, Hector could burn the Achaeans' fleet and decimate what was left of Agamemnon's invading forces.

JESUS

You know Homer and I do not. Later, I will take the time to gain that advantage. However, could you possibly cite for me something from Homer that would support your view? I am very interested in seeing if behind the image of Justice there is its idea of God.

SOCRATES

To believe one is honored, living under the influence of their God's Justice, gives the believer the voice to make a prophetic claim. If justice vindicates an injustice, the God that justifies the action is equally unjust. Surely, we would quickly add that such a view of God is no God at all nor can the hero be heroic. For no God would abandon the just nor would the just feel abandoned by their God.

JESUS

As I consider the enormity of what you have said, I would appreciate hearing something from Homer that might support this theological and ethical claim.

SOCRATES

That is a fair request. I am not word-perfect on what you need to hear. However, I will share with you my understanding of it. Achilles said that the justice of Zeus honored him and he believed this would sustain him through the closing act of the war. He said he would be safe by his black ship as the fury of Hector was unleashed. Achilles believed that Justice would sustain him while Hector's Trojan forces would crush the Achaeans. He believed he foresaw that Hector would break off his final attack and that would allow him to sail back to his homeland, Ithaca.

JESUS

Clearly, Achilles' idea of Justice and that of Zeus are intertwined. Your remarks force me to ask why Homer wrote the *Odyssey*. He has two different kinds of heroes, one Achilles, and the other, Odysseus. You have shown Achilles had to solve his problem before he could function heroically, but what was Odysseus' problem? Is there some bond that links them?

SOCRATES

So, for that, we will have to return to those discussions I have had with my circle of sages, as I call them. Shall I review Palamedes' role in these talks about Homer? He did play a major role in understanding that drama.

JESUS

The last should fill in the gaps in our talk. I know little about him. Is it possible that he has played a decisive role in all this?

SOCRATES

Yes, his role is central, but in a curious way. To understand his role we need to discuss Penelope, the wife of Odysseus. No easy task lies ahead of us because that means we have to discuss the journey of Odysseus.

JESUS

I would like that and in return I will share with you the meaning behind the *Gnostic Book of John*.

SOCRATES

I look forward to that exchange. To open up the meaning of Homer often requires discussing principles of our philosophy. If we can review a few of them, it will help us share the meaning behind these works.

JESUS

How can I refuse such an offer as this? You make my day and I am sure it will bring a smile along with it.

SOCRATES

The point of departure will be a truth that extends to all living things that possess Mind. Consider, after victory comes the inevitable counterattack. With the victory comes a new self-image that is in stark contrast to the older image. The older has been crafted from the pathologos and core beliefs. It is like a private and personal family-clan religion. The power it possesses is immense and survives human death in the land of Hades. To see this, it is possible to forge ahead with the urge to bring integrity into every act. Consider, as Odysseus entered Ithaca and the drama played out, it is possible to see that his mode of being differed from his past. He waits for the proper occasion to show himself as one who possesses the integrity of what it is to truly be a man. There may be others called wise, but he stands half again wiser than them all. Homer wants to present the wise as having problems and to show what it takes for the wise to overcome them.

JESUS

I would like to see that more fully. I do like what you have said and it has moved me deeply, but for all that, I would like to know more about what you discovered in these discussions.

SOCRATES

It will take us several steps, but I know with your own sincerity we will be able to share what was shared with me. So let me say at first that to achieve the victory, the old had to be submerged. With the victory, the old resurfaces and plagues the hero unless it is effectively dealt with. All of the troubles Odysseus faces with his crew before his journey into the House of Hades are manifestations of those very problems. To go home, to Ithaca, means to return as the hero without those core beliefs that undermine the Self. Before he entered the House of Hades, he had to recall vividly the tragedy of the Trojan War to the noble audience of Phaeacians. They in turn shared with Odysseus the meaning of the war and all else. He was told that all that he went through was the unfoldment of the Will of Zeus.

Zeus designed the war as a model for man. Entering the House of Hades, Odysseus saw that all of whatever a soul identified with has vast power that continues until it plays itself out. He saw the ghost of Achilles still identified with being a warrior, and he saw the image would spin itself out until there was no longer any power left to propel it. What is this but the power of the pathologos and core beliefs that shape the soul of man? Upon returning to Ithaca, his wife, Penelope, tests him before she will share her bed and life with him. Since Odysseus had feigned illness to avoid the war, she wanted to be sure he did not return with another false image. She loved the man who could refuse to right a wrong that he knew was frivolous. As she tested him, he grew in stature. Her strategies overcame the number and power of her ill-fated suitors. She is heroic without entering the battle. She presents us with a new image of a hero that reaches furthermost in life's struggle to be oneself. She uses her mind creatively to overcome seemingly impossible odds and difficulties. In her, we see the feminine Hercules.

Jesus

Socrates, I am seeing a new kind of sage, a new kind of holiness, and for that I am very grateful. You say that Odysseus feigned illness to avoid combat. Did you learn that from Homer or from any of your discussions here in heaven?

Socrates

No, it is not from Homer, but from the sage, Palamedes. He is one of those who can successfully confront and turn around those who refuse to meet their destiny. He is able to find insightful ways to bring a reversal by cutting through their defenses in simple and dramatic ways. The sage Palamedes did this when Odysseus feigned illness to avoid the expedition to Troy.

Jesus

No small feat, I would say. I will look into that very thing. Surely, his art is needed in many places with many people. I can see and appreciate these discussions that you had with these sages. I would like to return to those Gnostic texts that were recently discovered in Egypt. I mentioned them, and now I would like to see if they might function in the sage circle you have mentioned, or whether they are members of my circle.

Socrates

Egypt would be the place where treasures are likely to be found. They were ancient when the Hellenes were not, and they continued when we crumbled under the cruel forces of history. I do hope there will be another cave discovered filled with the treasures of our people, since so much has been lost and destroyed by irrational forces.

Jesus

What I found among these Gnostic texts is intertwined with their own interpretations of the Hebrew Bible. However, some of these interpretations reflect an ongoing problem that is best to set out. The problem is to understand the impact of your Hellenic thought upon these Gnostic authors. Surely they sought a way to Hellenize Judaism.

The Gnostic *Secret Book of John* is an attempt to reconcile the goodness of God with the existence of evil. John uses an interpretation of the Adam and Eve tale for this reconciliation. In the same way, he interprets away the meaning of Sophia as Wisdom so that it can play the role of the fallen angel.

SOCRATES

There it is again. When believers grasp the power that understanding can bring through the use of analogies and allegories, they experience a desperate effort to hold onto their own core beliefs. They suffer by seeing the comparison and try in every way to find parallels between the new Hellenic ideas with their own core beliefs. As we have seen, the effort lacks the power to transform the old into the new. The failure creates the need for a counter force to save the core beliefs. This need to block this Hellenization drives believers to create a bond with the old believers and form small, closed communities. However, when they do accept the challenge to reformulate the old in terms of the emerging *Logos*, it changes the character and vision of their believers into an awakening community without the walls of closed-minded beliefs.

JESUS

True, but the church and temple could offer an alternative to clan leadership. The bridge from the irrational family-clan beliefs to humanness is through a rational spiritual belief in the promise of man's enlightenment. The danger is when the core beliefs of the clan mirror or support that of their religion. The mindless ones follow any call to duty and they leave in their wake chaos and destruction. The ignorant follow the leader and then blame him for whatever failures follow from his leadership. It keeps them from seeing their own crimes against the dignity of their fellow man. They plead that they are innocent and cry aloud that they were only doing their duty. The cry of doing one's duty blinds them from seeing themselves. We call this the unleashing of the tyranny of the mindless many.

Chorus

Here it is as plain as can be. This is nothing but the rejection of tradition in favor of an emptiness of disbelief. Here it is. We finally got a religion we can believe in and these guys come along and try to destroy what they can't believe. The burden of sin and suffering is too terrible to bear. The church offers a way to get out of the intolerable weight of sin. We finally got a religion we need, and they come along to try to make it rational. Who cares if it is rational? Forget their boast because it is nothing other than another attack by these phony intellectuals against us. Do away with punishment and the bad guys smile away. The only thing that keeps them even a little bit in line is the fear of punishment. As for the Will of Zeus, well, you have to be kidding. How can a fiction have a will? There is nothing worthwhile here, nothing. It is just a play so you can laugh your way through it.

Anti-Chorus

The religion that you can believe in needs to uplift you into the next phase in your spiritual path, not fortify your ignorance against change. The idea that punishment keeps some from doing the bad is not as important as recognizing that what it really does is to force people to find ways to escape being caught. You know, I think that even the idea of sin needs to be looked at. It really means one has missed the mark, as in archery. What you need when you miss the mark, or target, is to discover your fault and correct it. What would it take to get you to listen to what is going on here?

SOCRATES

True it is that it is your turn to share what you see among these texts. Which among them is closest to your own teachings?

JESUS

It is not an easy task. I could approach it like you do. It would make it easy if I were to do that.

SOCRATES

I am for it, but what is the problem you see in stating it directly and simply?

JESUS

Your skill in words includes finding general themes in a jumble of differences, that's what.

SOCRATES

Please go on and then I might respond to whatever you say.

JESUS

Now, that is an offer I cannot refuse. Then let me take the Gnostic works we mentioned and take the *Secret Book of John* for our analysis. The work surfaces the fundamental problem of the Hebrew Bible. The importance of the work is obvious, yet its meaning is obscure. To bring understanding to it is very difficult because its stories are merely stated as primal events. Consider: these events have little if any capacity to generalize. We could call them idiosyncratic since they stand with singular importance without any transparent meaning. Thus, attempts to draw meaning from them are very difficult if not impossible. These stories become easy targets for interpretation since by themselves they are unique. Equally, the major ideas within these works are like the stories, difficult to blend into a unity since they are not linked together for hierarchical sets of meaning. Believers are left with either finding some interpretations or remaining silent.

Socrates

You need to bring the light into the dark shadows of night to see what stands behind those fleeting images.

Jesus

That is fair. The Adam and Eve theme plays a major role in Gnostic John's work as it does in some others, but here it makes visible the problem of interpretation in the clearest of terms. The story itself is simple, but for meaning, it is all but invisible. The work itself clearly says that God does not exile and punish Adam and Eve for what they did. No, only Adam is sent out of the Garden of Eden to till the soil from which he was created. Surely, that must be a sacred place. Again, there are Gods in this story, not one, but many. The God that speaks out is jealous after discovering they have eaten of the Tree of the Knowledge of Good and Evil. He says he fears that they may reach out and eat of the Tree of Life and become "like one of us," immortal. This possibility drives God's anger. He is jealous that man might become a God and become immortal. It is this possibility that drives the story. Clearly, there is no punishment for either Adam or Eve. Eve is not mentioned as leaving the Garden, so she was not sent out of the Garden with Adam. God's jealousy carries the weight of sin. For, it must be a sin to block those who might benefit by eating of the Tree of Life. The story is simple and it has an internal integrity, as you would call it, but to find it takes a bit of reasoning and a departure from interpretation.

SOCRATES

Really, I would like to hear what you have found about its integrity.

JESUS

I would rather you do it. I'll set it out and you do the work. List all the characters in the story; single out each of their remarks that have any futurity, or prediction, to them. We can then see if what they expect will be confirmed in the story itself. After you do this, you must tell me how well the roles of the characters form into a unity that is truly prophetic.

SOCRATES

Already I see how this might change my view of that story. I will do as you say. I expect you could say the same about the other stories from the Hebrew Bible that Gnostic John uses in his work. Does he also add a system to the ideas you mentioned that you say were isolated and lacking union?

JESUS

Yes. To express what he accepts as my true vision, he uses ideas from Hellenic thought and from the Prometheus legend, like forethought, afterthought, and the power of Mind. He also brings into his work the idea of perfect Mind as having foreknowledge of itself. It emerges from the will of the spirit. Sure enough, here we see echoes of Athena's birth from the Mind of Zeus. John also adds the idea of triads to his work. We both know that the idea of a triad is fundamental because if a duad were basic, it would be without love and there would be no true intimacy.

SOCRATES

It is pleasant to talk about this and smile at our sameness, is it not? Down the line of those like me, there is an interpreter of mine,

Proclus, who cultivated his philosophy on this very idea of the triad. It is the principle found in his thought, and it is the basis of the mean analogy. He noted it was the characteristic idea of every divine order, and he revealed its inner dynamic expressed as principles of order and symmetry, which are expressed as and within the mean analogy.

Jesus

To know Beauty is enough, they say, but to understand her triadic principles is to understand her intrinsic intelligibility and source of strength and power.

Socrates

Yes, indeed, that is so. Further, recall we agreed that anything that is said to have an existence and power is also said to have some activity that follows from that power. So, existence, power and activity are the three ideas brought together into a unity and the unity is called the triad. With this idea of the triad, other terms can be substituted, but they must share those characteristics. From what you are saying, I can expect that you found John uses triads without the fitness they should have.

Jesus

Yes, that is true. John also discusses the hierarchy of ideas, without demonstrating their necessary placement and order, so it lacks the unity of ideas that you indicate it should have. He uses the noblest of ideas, the One, and calls it Father, and another time calls it Light, and equally he does the same with the ideas of Mother and Child, without carefully preserving their key differences or internal integrity.

Socrates

The meanings behind the idea of the metaphor, Father, does not even approach that of describing Pure Being, or the realm of the Intelligible, much less the Good, or the One itself. Yet, as we know, the idea of Father is an essential part of those ideas we call core beliefs. If the higher range of meanings of Father does not include such ideas as the Good, the most brilliant light of Being, or the perfection of Beauty Itself, or Truth, then the idea of Father lacks a richness it is capable of expressing.

JESUS

Does the length of a man's shadow measure the man? Now, where do these ideas emerge among your followers?

SOCRATES

Thank you for the invitation. Among our philosophers, Iamblichus, Plotinus, and Proclus have brought our philosophy along more contemplative and metaphysical and reflective lines. Among them, Plotinus offers a banquet of philosophical ideas that raise the level of reflection to the psychic states of mind as well as bringing additional clarity to metaphysical ideas. He views the Soul, Love, Beauty, and Contemplation through his contemplative philosophical experiences. It is through his experiences that he is able to present Mind understanding the Mind. His philosophy is the cultivation of the mystic experience of the divine luminosity, but without a corresponding dialectic his works lack a true unity of our philosophy. When he describes his dialectic, it lacks the scope and precision of Plato's dialectic, as well as that of Proclus.

In a similar way, these philosophers did not explore the dream world. We could say they advanced the metaphysics in a remarkable way and brought more of the personal element of their experience into our philosophy. However, as a group, they do not include the study of dreams or midwifery for the soul.

JESUS

Well, let's call them a new member of the class of interpreters. For clearly they advance certain parts of philosophy and ignore other important parts.

SOCRATES

What you say is true, because what Proclus advanced was a beautiful exploration of our metaphysics, and he also authored a divine vision of the elements of theology. He opened up several of Plato's dialogues and certainly advanced the dialectic, as you said. However, he did another great service; he showed the rational structure of his metaphysics matched and had exact correspondences with our Hellenic account of the Gods.

JESUS

Yes, indeed, he has a place of honor among us. It is clear that your followers went on even further to develop your way of doing philosophy, but mine ended soon after it became set in stone by the church. I am interested in these followers of yours and would like to return to them after we have explored a puzzling question that I have of your own philosophy. Have any of these later philosophers reached the final stage of your philosophy? If not, could you explain where they still need to go to develop further or what is needed to bring it to its fullness?

SOCRATES

Let's see what you are asking. It is not a simple task, but with Truth as our guide, I must oblige you. Since the work that is the cornerstone of all these followers of mine is Plato's *Parmenides*, I shall follow their lead and be guided by the same approach. We will need the last philosopher of the Athenian Academy, Damascius, whose teaching at the Academy ended when the Christian Emperor

Justinian closed down the schools of philosophy in 529. I have already mentioned that Plato clearly stated that it was through dreams that I received insights into the divine. He went on to say that it was through oracles and dreams that I was commanded by the God to follow my practice. Most importantly, he said it was through dreams that one can recover what one does not know about one's own past, present and future. However, he did not, nor did those who followed him, stress the philosophical significance that the role of dreams plays in human destiny. His understanding adds much to the primary riddles philosophy seeks to understand and experience.

The primary ideas of our philosophy are the One, or the Good, the Idea of the Good, or that brilliant light of Being, and the Soul, or the nature of the Soul. The problem, of course, we fully appreciate. For, if the One is beyond all categories or qualities, how is it the source of that which can only be described with superlative categories and qualities?

Equally, how can that which is a union of all these categories and qualities be the source of that which is fragmented into an innumerable manyness?

Now, add to that the idea in our philosophy that there can be a return from that manyness to the One.

The philosophical quest is for each soul to make the journey to that source of all sources. The effort to render some rational account of these problems is one of the goals of philosophy. It is not just for cleaning up metaphysical problems, because this kind of reflection is the meditation that leads to the doorway of spiritual vision.

Jesus

How could I possibly disagree? Certainly, these are the ideas for both of us, our work and practice. I say that because my followers stress the need to believe in the primary triad of Father, Son, and

Spirit. At this point it may be that there is only a slight difference between your use and mine of these ideas. What, then, are the ways that Damascius links these ideas together? Can I expect that Damascius had a major place in his philosophy for the nature of dreams? I ask that because of the importance you place on the study of dreams.

Socrates

No, he did not, even though he did see that dreams, like divine visions, are truthful. I heard this from the sage Orpheus. He said that Damascius recognized that the eternal inner spark of the divine pours itself out in its full glory, out-dazzling the world of becoming. Is it not interesting that Damascius acknowledged that the divine luminosity could be fully realized in dreams? Surely, while that is a major insight into the role of dreams and inner visions from the realm of the Intelligible, he did not bring this insight into his system as a whole.

Jesus

If he had made a place for it within his philosophy, would it have brought his own thought into a higher unity, and could it add to the puzzle of the relationship between the Soul and the Intelligible, or the Intellect? Still, he did advance your system, so he is among those who have confirmed your vision, and he can be added to those who advance your work. It is no small thing that he added that divine luminosity also comes in dreams. As you know, I have a keen interest in this subject, as I know you do since we both have entered into that divine luminosity.

Socrates

Yes, Jesus, you are correct about that. These problems that I mentioned are interrelated, so gaining an insight into one may afford another insight into the others. But, before we go forward it would be best to first open up and discuss just what this problem is. Then we can see if what I put forward will allow us to say the puzzle has either been solved or that we have advanced it a step in that direction. Would you say that is a fair way of going? If so, we may return to Plato's *Parmenides*.

JESUS

You do mention Parmenides quite often and that leads me to ask you: if he had a teacher, who was he?

SOCRATES

Xenophanes of Colophon was his teacher and it was he who held that God is One. He said that it is the whole of God that sees, hears, and thinks. There were those who sought to see that very thing in themselves. They went around and asked themselves those very things and it was this that brought them to philosophy. Staying with these sayings throughout their life, they came to see that the mystery behind those sayings can be actually realized, and in that realization they saw what must be seen. He started what Parmenides developed into a very profound system of thought. It became the object of contemplation for many.

JESUS

Yes, it is good. I would enjoy seeing how Plato's *Parmenides* can be used to both open up this problem, and through it to see its possible solution.

SOCRATES

First, then, shall we agree that there is something in human beings that not only has life but also something within that ponders, reflects, and is aware of itself? I ask that because since it has those ways of being, it also can act and do what it does and so achieves what it can.

JESUS

Sure thing. I can go along with that. What else do you need to go further?

SOCRATES

Well, it allows us to say that within man there is something that can revert upon itself and from that an activity can emerge. Or, simply, we can say the mark of being a living person is to have this power of reversion as well as the ability to act. A more philosophical way of saying this is to say that the distinctive mark of the soul of man is that it has what the Greeks called *ousia*, or substance and activity. Again, we should say that this idea of activity must include an activity that manifests the fullest flowering of the human spirit, or soul. Now, we need to see these two ideas in the study of the nature of dreams, and to do that we should first explore the dynamics of dreams.

JESUS

Again, I like the way you are going. You separate the dynamics of dreams from the nature of dreams. Good. You could explain what you are about to do, but I wonder if you would take me along the path through dialogue. I would appreciate that because taking each step along the way will allow me the chance to reflect and to see it for myself. If so, could you say something about your use of the idea of dreams having a nature?

SOCRATES

Good question there, Jesus. To answer it requires we take a dialogical trip into what is common to all dreams. Since we have

discussed dreams before, can we now say that dreams show a kind
of unusual intelligence?

JESUS

From what you have said, I would say that if dreams are reflected
upon in a non-interpretive way, then they show a pattern of being
part of a rational order.

SOCRATES

Does it appear to you that the dream comes at the right time
for the dreamer to reflect and learn from? Further, what kind of
knowledge must the "Dream Maker" have of each dreamer for the
dream to match the spiritual life of the dreamer?

JESUS

I like those questions because it causes me to reflect back upon
the meaning of what you have said about dreams. From what we
have agreed to, I can only say that the Dream Maker must have an
intimate knowledge of the problems the dreamer faces, even when
the dreamer is not aware of the kind of problem they are facing.
So what can I say but that the maker of dreams far excels in intelligence that of the dreamer. What I find intriguing is the beauty
of the simplicity of the dream messages. It condenses so much in a
few sentences and with just a few images. It is very insightful and
beautiful the way the Dream Maker fashions the dreams.

SOCRATES

Yes, it has all those features, and yet another remarkable dimension is present in dreams. It is through the power of dreams that the
dreamer is brought to make connections between his or her present
problem and its roots in early childhood experiences. Dreams also
often include scenes of high and low states of mind, or emotional states.

In exploring the high states, the full content becomes visible, surfacing the presence of more profound states of mind of the dream. In a similar way, opening up the low states can bring the dreamer to find parallels to that experience in the dreamer's past. In recalling the dream, the dreamer is given the opportunity to recall additional material that the dreamer had forgotten.

Jesus

You are bringing the Logos to dreams. So this is the way you uncover enlightenment experiences that have been forgotten or have been ignored or forgotten by the dreamer.

Socrates

It is one thing to have the taste of enlightenment and another to be in full union with it. Upon analysis, the briefest state that could have easily been overlooked can bring insight into the nature of the Self and Reality. To remain in that state and discover its depth brings the Mind to realize why it is that the pure light of divine luminosity is a dynamic presence. The dynamic, as we both know, is the Mind turning upon itself. Some of the powers of the Mind can then be unfolded and expressed.

Jesus

Yes, it is as you say, and wondrous it is to be sharing it and exploring its depth. Truly it is a bountiful gift beyond all else. For the Mind to know itself through dreams is remarkable as is the depth of knowledge it transmits.

Socrates

It is as you say. For the Dream Maker has an astonishing knowledge of the dreamer. It must know their spiritual path and what stage the dreamer is in for the dream to have the impact it has. The

Dream Maker must have, as it were, a spiritual map within which to fix each soul's struggle and knows what is needed to bring the dreamer to realize the blocks they face.

JESUS

It is the most profound of knowledge and reaches as far as the boundary of experience. In what terms do you describe it?

SOCRATES

To benefit the soul in this way means the Dream Maker must possess an art of dreams. To possess a knowledge that understands the present plight of the dreamer, and offers a way to resolve that problem for the betterment of the dreamer, means the Dream Maker possess an art. Here we can see the doctor of the soul at work, making a diagnosis of the soul's condition, presenting the soul with the means for its own treatment, and bringing the soul to understand the art. For this way of doing philosophy initiates the dreamer into the questions that can revert the Mind to explore the Mind in the most meaningful way. The same or similar questions can be carefully applied to all dreams. The questions are a pathway into the mysteries of the Mind as it unlocks its secrets.

JESUS

No answers, only questions. I like the idea of a question since it means one is on a quest.

SOCRATES

To keep a question and to ponder it and not let go of it is the doorway into the true life of the soul. The craftsman of dreams only gives the dreamer the materials for the dreamer to reflect upon and to ponder. The task of the dreamer is to bring together all it has understood into a unity. What does this mean? Pondering and reflecting on dreams awakens a recursive intellectual ability that matures as it is cultivated. The content of the dream is the activity drawn from the life of the dreamer for contemplation. The dream comes while we sleep so that it emerges from the darkness of sleep into the light of the dream and passes again into that darkness. Upon awakening, as we revert upon it and reflect, it becomes an object of contemplation.

Jesus

Out of the silence comes a voice worthy of pondering. Surely, that is the same as in other things, isn't it?

Socrates

Very true, because the same dynamics mark the very nature of our existence. We can easily see it in the waking life of man. For as each thought emerges, it quickly returns to an emptiness, so in the same way, it is out of this emptiness that each perception and thought is framed between successive states of emptiness. This emptiness is only an instant. The instant is followed by the moment called the now and followed again by another instant.

Jesus

Then the instant is all that is and it is in front of us. The mystery is right here. Among your followers, who was it that set this out for our reflections?

Socrates

The first formulation of it must have been some time in the past, but it does appear as the third hypothesis of Plato's *Parmenides*. Each successive moment surfaces what is most proper and due in the present event. In that moment of instantaneousness, which has no qualities, comes all that is needed for the next moment's change and development. The mystery of where the source of change and motion comes from is right here in front of us. It takes place in no time and without changing, yet it is the source of both change and development. It is out of the instant that the moment of experience arrives and returns to its source.

JESUS

And it must fit perfectly and be in harmony with all that has happened in that past moment. Now, for it to fit so smoothly with the past moment means its astonishing precision must be the result of an extraordinary craftsman.

SOCRATES

Yes, and it must have an internal integrity of vast proportion; it must fit most precisely the past conditions of each thing, each thought and perception. And, the name of the craftsman is, of course, the Logos. However, beyond that, it carries the wishes and goals of the dreamer into the next moment.

JESUS

"That without any qualities" sounds like another idea that was raised earlier, the One. Since you have returned to it, it may fit even more. So could you count this as a possible way of answering the riddle of how the One becomes many?

SOCRATES

As it is said, if relations are constant and terms vary, then you may have one dynamic throughout. So, we just might say that in a similar way whatever springs from an emptiness and returns has the marks of generation. If the "many" is all that is, and moreover, to say it has sprung in some mysterious way from the One, how can we say that the One and many are successive so that in becoming

One its being the many is let go, and when being many the One vanishes? For in becoming both One and many and in time it passes through the instantaneous that does not exist in time, but into this and out from this the two dance the sacred dance we philosophers often call Parmenides' third song, his third hypothesis. It is between successive instants that the gap becomes the source of all change.

Jesus

The melody of that song runs through many sacred things. I am very pleased to hear of this. The gap is surely a most noble expression for the Intelligible Logos that binds together all things and is the source of all.

Socrates

Yes, the gap does not have a temporal existence, but it is through it that the continuity of each thing is assured. It is through this that the next event has been shaped to uniquely fit into the moment. We can say that this process brings into a unity all that is, and it brings to it the next phase of its existence in the most perfect way.

Jesus

The moment has been unified as perfectly as an art can give birth to its proper excellence. Then the creative dynamic must reach into the most fundamental mode of existence of what truly is.

Socrates

That is true because within the moment it is possible to act, and in acting, we affect that Reality which underlies all that is, and it is this that changes through our reflections and contemplations, and carries the soul along, assuring our particular spiritual growth and development. We call it *ousia*, though some people call it substance, yet that word, substance, does not carry all the meanings we have found that are central to the idea of *ousia*. Both *ousia* and the activity that springs from it form a unity.

JESUS

Yes, the idea of the instant is what several of my followers have called the gap, the moment of mystery. Your followers have gone further because of your deep interest in understanding since this is what shapes one's own inner experience.

SOCRATES

In the gap, as it were, there is the intelligence that instantaneously reverts upon the map of all spiritual development and identifies each soul and thing providing for its continuity with its next step in its path to fulfilling its destiny.

JESUS

And shall I add that the whole shines through under the banner of Justice?

SOCRATES

Yes, that is very true as Truth is the hallmark of creation. Now, we can say that each moment has been brought into existence through a supremely vast Intelligence recursively functioning in a unified way for the unfolding of the Cosmos, and as such, it reflects the higher principles in every microsecond. The uniting power from which it has emerged is the creative activity we call *ousia*. The unified itself is the shadow of the One itself.

JESUS

Well, Socrates, it is good to see that your philosophy reflects the power of that Intelligence and that your study of dreams confirms your philosophy in a personally unique way. Then the One becomes the all as the all becomes the One. Splendid it is.

SOCRATES

Well said, Jesus, well said. The becoming proceeds and returns as it reflects the Intelligible order. The Intelligence we speak of has another name that we both enjoy hearing, and that is Mind itself, is it not?

JESUS

Very true it is, Socrates. Once more, who among your followers has come closest in advancing this philosophy of yours?

SOCRATES

A crown needs to be placed on Damascius, but not for the highest office. He has reflected on all those philosophers we mentioned. Behind it all he saw a Reality that can be expressed as the One, the Unified, the reflecting *ousia*, and the activity that has given birth to our Cosmos. He expressed a high value for dreams but had not seen how to bring them into his system of philosophy. Surely, there will be others along the way who will go further.

JESUS

We have reached an interesting point, and to go the next step will delight us both. I have been wondering about this for a while now. Tell me, Socrates, how will we decide if a follower is yours or mine?

SOCRATES

Now that is an interesting question. Your point is well made, and it may be that it will decide much if it turns out that the follower you are going to mention is shared by us both. Could there be another possibility? What if this new follower of yours turns out to have a view that goes beyond both of our positions? Then, surely, we will both be the followers of this new candidate, won't we?

Jesus

We have our divisions, don't we? What follows if there is room for another?

Socrates

It is no small thing you are asking. If there is a new category, it just may doom all the others. What you are proposing must mean you have a vision of a new kind of metaphysics and, just maybe, a new philosophy.

Jesus

I like what you do. You raise the issue to a higher level. Then I will have to be careful how to best represent this candidate, as you call him. I do think I have a way of going. What if I cite the major ideas of our candidate and you tell me if he belongs in your camp or mine? Surely, that means I will have to do justice to what I select and offer it to you for your comments. So, then, let me ask you: if a new idea of man is brought forward that clearly announces a new kind of "divine-manlike activity," would not that mean that the divine, or God, has made man to no longer reflect upon himself as man, but as a God whose activity is in the sphere of the new man?

Socrates

What is going on here? You are approaching this problem as I would have liked to. You single out the idea of activity that we have discussed and link it to a very profound idea. I am always cautious about the use of the term God, but here you advance it under the banner of our new candidate. Is it equally certain that your source also advances the idea of *ousia*, or substance, in the way we have discussed it?

JESUS

You are correct in that because he does use the idea *ousia*, or substance. The mystery of the identity of our candidate can be further deepened if I share with you his understanding of this remarkable term, *ousia*.

SOCRATES

Please do that. I am more than amazed and wait to hear more. I agree this term is essential to our philosophy, and to learn more of its meaning would delight me.

JESUS

If the idea of goodness and even of godliness merely suggests that the Good and God are their source, you will fail to grasp what *ousia* is. Why? Because it is the power of *ousia's* reversion that makes others good and godlike while their source is beyond the very idea of source. It is this essential divine substance, or *ousia*, that has taken on an existence in our world.

SOCRATES

However, if it takes on an existence among us, then by what means does it accomplish this?

JESUS

It is that which in man has been concealed and is now present as we enter into its secret ways of being.

SOCRATES

Well, there is nothing I can say about this; I applaud to the skies
what you are saying.

JESUS

As you have said, the power of *ousia* brings us to reflect and turn
about, and that begins the awakening of the inner life of philosophy.
The Good, or the One, is no longer conceived of as remote and
transcendent, but near and most essential to us. Everywhere we
reach out to experience we always discriminate a oneness of this or
that. Without this ability there would be no intellectual life and
no reflection. So, you ask, what shall we say of it? The One shows
itself in everything; as we reach out to experience we do so because
we think it good to do so. The Good, which we also call the One, is
part-and-parcel of all we experience and it is through the power of
ousia we realize we are not strangers to the divine. By the intelligence
that functions in and through the gap there appears the moment, an
instantaneous event. It is this that you have spoken of many times
and it emerges from the gap. For it is this that surrounds whatever
is, yet it is not in time and, so, is also timeless. From its prior pure
state it has entered the world and is the very substance of our growth
and of change in all things.

SOCRATES

Has this candidate of yours said that God dwells invisibly by
his own excessive brilliance in the divine luminosity? And does he
say that those who are worthy come to know and see God through
that very divine luminosity?

JESUS

Well, Socrates, he has not been hidden from you. Yes, it has
been said that Dionysius was Paul's companion. Yes, he is the one

who urges us to speak in defense of the Truth and that means, does it not, doing what we are now doing?

SOCRATES

If it is as you say, Dionysius, who we have called the Areopagite, had instructed those about him on the principles of the dialectic. Is it not likely that you have learned this art yourself and have hidden it from me?

JESUS

A pause often refreshes the soul, does it not? So, then, let me in turn ask you if you understand what this Dionysius has said about me? Then would you not say that you have come to see me as he saw me? Now, what does that make you, my dear Socrates?

SOCRATES

I am not far off if I say you either learn very quickly or you have had this dialectical ability all along. So what shall I say? Before I say what I think, I would rather have you discuss further what you can say about our friend, Dionysius the Areopagite. I would like you to review whatever you have seen about his idea of the dialectic, or logic.

Recall that in Mark's Gospel the keys to solving the esoteric parables for the passage to the Kingdom of God were limited to the inner circle of disciples and their colleagues. The Kingdom was not in Heaven, but on Earth, not in the future, but in the present. It is the result of training the mind to see a solution into each parable.

For Dionysius the Areopagite, the Kingdom of God is open to those capable of participating in it. The experience itself is that of grasping Truth and Reality. It unfolds a well-being and goodness from the Good. Clearly, Dionysius expresses this idea of the Kingdom of God into a higher, more cosmic philosophical idea, and in this movement he brings his idea of Christianity into a Platonic vision of Reality. His vision is deeply indebted to Proclus, and he brought into existence a way to understand the transfiguration and how that experience links all those philosophical terms into a unity. Dionysius' writings gave the opportunity to embrace reason and understanding as the natural corollaries to mystical experience.

CHORUS

You need to laugh at this so-called analysis. They are agreeing with the absurd. Imagine for a moment that Mark's Gospel rejects Paul and no one sees it but these two. Why believe it? It is all a matter of faith. I believe it because it is beyond the reach of these intellectuals' phony criticism. I can only warn you against this stuff. Parmenides again and again? Why don't they dump what no one finds meaningful? Then, they appeal to Gnostic John for support. How can a heretic like Gnostic John support Christianity? I'll tell you straight. Sure, Plato's Academy and the other pagan schools of philosophy were closed down, and there is no need to open them up again. Frankly, when a sword is over your head, you'll switch, because whatever you believe in is just as good as anything else.

ANTI-CHORUS

The idea of closing down the Academy appeals to you because you can't stand differences, can you? You want things simple and hate the complex. Life is complex; look around and you'll see that. Look into the souls of those about you and you can see the desperate plea for understanding not only oneself, but also the nature of Reality. You don't want to see what is right in front of you, so you create this mask of yours and make believe that you are making sense by defending what you don't understand.

SOCRATES

Now, I have a curious question about the way you communicate with your followers. Here it is. It turns out that you can and do follow these philosophical riddles. You follow and enjoy taking on the path of the dialectic. This kind of thinking you do not share with your followers. Why? You use parables and confront your followers with wakeup calls. Is there a reason you prefer to use those devices?

JESUS

If you were to select one of the sentences I just used as an example of this kind of thinking, what would you select?

SOCRATES

Well, Jesus, I don't need a sentence for that since all I need is the Idea of the Good or of the One Self.

JESUS

Thanks, Socrates, you made my task so much the easier. Now, can you share those ideas with another without using the definite article, "the"?

SOCRATES

No, I don't think that is possible without the article. If I substitute the word "that" for "the," then it loses its key meaning.

JESUS

Another thing, do you notice that both the ideas of good and one are adjectives that are used to qualify some particular noun? But with the article "the," it transforms an adjective into a substantive, or into a noun. The power of that article makes the adjective into a substantive that has the widest scope and refers to the most fundamental of things.

The indefinite article is singular: a one-out-of-many, or "a" good. However, with the definite article, "the," it is singular in a different way than the indefinite article "a." With the definite article, it becomes that which is only one, but it is above all others, has an existence, and is the foundation for other key terms, such as the Good.

SOCRATES

This is the magic of some languages.

JESUS

I see that you are referring to the Hebrew language. They have no word for the indefinite article, "a." They do have the demonstrative pronoun, whose mark always has specificity and cannot carry the meaning of the definite article, "the." The demonstrative pronoun is often translated as "that" and sometimes as "the" as when one is pointing out something, such as "a" or "that" boy.

SOCRATES

Are you saying that the Hebrew language does not have this magical term? Good heavens! That must mean such a language will have great difficulty fully comprehending our Hellenic philosophy. If you can't express it, you can't think it. This would tend to make people more concrete or focused on the moment rather than explore the source of all sources. The result would focus people's interest in doing particular things, becoming more concrete in their thinking, and through this avoidance miss out on the power of language for reflection. It just might account for the hostility some people experience from others when they seek to go beyond the concrete view of Reality. Their entry into our Hellenic thought would be handicapped without the study of Greek, wouldn't it?

JESUS

True, but the use of parables would awaken the Mind to turn upon itself. It would turn them about and bring them to wonder, and they would enter into that silence out of which wonder creates the passage to more profound states of mind.

Socrates

Yes, and equally through languages that contain this gift, it would make the passage to philosophy and our theology much easier to enter into, wouldn't it? I wonder what language has the greatest power to represent most fairly our theology and philosophy.

Jesus

The well-known inherent difficulties or shortcomings of Hebrew exclude it from doing this kind of philosophy; without a "the" they are out.

Socrates

With a perfect language expressing the purest and most complete philosophy, you would have secured a way to express ones most profound thoughts.

Jesus

I agree, but what is more important to me is whether it would bring man to a higher and more profound way of Being. Those I taught lived in a bilingual area, Decapolis, and Galilee, speaking Greek and a few speaking Hebrew. Then the Gnostic thinkers we have discussed must have been Greek speaking and shared in its culture.

Socrates

Well, there is the hope that with the realization of the integrity of the Cosmos that man will become more rational and open to more significant aspects of philosophical life.

JESUS

In what terms do you understand the conflicts of those cave dwellers? They may be like those I leave only with parables, but I do explain their meaning to those in my inner circle.

SOCRATES

Cave dwellers, as we call them, are victims of having learned false beliefs of the Self and Reality. They are guardians of those beliefs and loyal to those who transmitted that pseudo-learning. Without philosophical goals, they seek power, money, and empty pleasures.

JESUS

You say it loud and clear, Socrates, but from what I have heard, you are no stranger to pleasures. You urge your followers to avoid what you indulge in. At least, that is what I have heard.

SOCRATES

Now, Jesus, shouldn't you first tell me what you have heard? How can I defend myself or offer explanations when you haven't said what I have violated?

JESUS

True enough, but your followers have a feud with the body and devote much worry and effort to overcome the desires of the body and among those desires the uppermost are those of sexual experience. You did contribute to this problem because you teach one thing and live another. As you have said, you fathered a child when you were over seventy years of age. What do you make of this? I could add that some who seek the spiritual life flee to monasteries and hermitages, but you have gone into these very things. You even gained distinction as a soldier in a military campaign. I have heard you also drank others under the table and went home after a drinking banquet as if you never had a drink yourself. Are you not different from your followers? What do you make of this difference?

SOCRATES

When whatever is done is done with the Mind's awareness of what it is that is being done then the Mind is free of any imposition of any fantasy. A soul doesn't desire because it desires, rather it desires only if it fits into what is thought to be good and real, but it is often mistaken about what its good is. When the mind is occupied with some illusion when it does what it does then the fantasy uses, as it were, the immediacy and the power of the act to enliven the fantasy. If the mind is occupied with some illusion when it does what it does, then the consequences will end up as a disaster.

Thus, there is nothing that brings greater harm than if one is mistaken as to what is True and Real. It is not what is done that is significant, but what state of mind accompanies whatever is done. Naturally, what is done should conform to one's ideal and not one's fantasy.

JESUS

So, you drink and make love with a pure Mind that is free of any imposition of false images, interesting. But that doesn't make it ideal, does it? What can be worse than to entertain thoughts one believes true and feels justified in acting them out without realizing that they are completely mistaken about the truth of what they believe?

SOCRATES

Again, you are right about that. To do what one does with a pure Mind must include that the very doing must fit nicely within what is your highest sense of being right and being just. Surely, it is very likely that without that sense of justice of one's acts and the recognition that it is consistent with one's philosophical goals, that one is harboring a false idea of what is Real and True. Many believe that their fantasy life is their own creation, but they fail to recognize the self-image within the fantasy is a manifestation of a false identification.

Jesus

Yes, and if one has been persuaded and encouraged to believe in such a false Idea of the Self or Reality, then they are doomed to being irrelevant.

Socrates

I have often stressed to those about me that to be ignorant about what is Real and True is what everyone hates and fears. There is nothing more important than having Truth as a companion to one's idea of Reality. The inner connection between what is considered good, the desire for it, and the quest for it, is important to see clearly. I have often called it the inner triad.

Jesus

That was good. Interesting comparison you have here. Mankind imitates creation in his own inner world. However, when it takes on the form of a daydream, then, if I may say so, all hell breaks loose. You know, of course, that many say your kind of philosophy is nothing other than entering and staying within a world of fantasy.

Socrates

Yes, the many do hurl that charge against us. They forget the difference between fantasy and philosophical speculation. In fantasy there is a false image of the Self, and its drama has no correspondence with the way to Truth of the meditation of the philosopher. The speculations of philosophy lead to an understanding and experience of the true Self, and that does not contain any element of the life of fantasy.

Jesus

So, the daydream and your kind of speculation both have a triadic structure. I had wondered if you were going to talk about the triad for all creation, the procession from the One, that which remains, and the return that all creation is said to be part of. I haven't heard much about it from you.

Socrates

Yes, some of my followers have expressed that very idea. But would you not agree, if anything were to proceed from the One, it wouldn't be a One, but it would have to have been a many since it would have been itself, a One, and what proceeded from it, right? Surely, if we count both the One and what proceeded from it, we would have not one but two things.

Jesus

Yes, that is right.

Socrates

Equally, if it returns, it would become a many since there would be the One and what returned to it. Surely, that would amount to at least two, or as many as return to it. What remains would be part of the three since from it something came forth, and what returned would also be part of a whole.

Jesus

Many of my interpreters have stressed that the highest or most profound interpretation of God must include that God exists; for if existence is not attributed to God, then what kind of God could there be? However, they do not discuss what kind of existence that would be.

SOCRATES

Yes, through these interpreters, you have raised the right question. The question is never going away since it is always a pressing concern. If we are to take a careful look at this question, we will need to ask about one word, "beyond." Consider, if I were to say that I saw something so beautiful that the word beautiful failed to do it justice, then it is likely that if no words could communicate that kind of experience, we could say that the experience of Beauty was beyond words. While we can wonder about this, would you not say that for the highest idea of God, no words or categories could be found to describe God? If so, then words would be wholly inadequate and there would be no possible description of such a God.

JESUS

Yes, that is so. I can recall experiences I have encountered that are beyond any words. Among experiences, those called transfiguration into divine luminosity are such as to be said to be beyond words.

SOCRATES

True, yet you would say that the experience of that divine luminosity was real and not an illusion, would you not?

JESUS

Yes to that.

SOCRATES

And would you not say that this idea of Real means that it truly exists?

Jesus

Yes again to that.

Socrates

However, if the idea of existence is added to it, like the One exists, then there would be something added to the idea of One other than itself and that would be existence, or what is, or "Is." There is a word called "Itself" that, strictly speaking, refers to nothing other than "Itself." It is used to refer to the highest idea of God, the One. In all fairness, even here we are saying that it is, just by itself. If we do that, then we are not talking about the One, rather we are contrasting it with something that can be just by itself.

Jesus

Then, to use your language, I would say that "One" is the only word to describe the profound nature of God.

Socrates

However, there must be a difference between this most lofty idea of God and the idea of the One, since the idea of One must be distinct, at least in some way or manner, from God. The idea of God includes the idea of existence, or Being, but not so the Good, or the One Self. Indeed, even calling this noblest idea of God a God limits the idea of God, since it must refer to something, and not something else, and that would mean it is not beyond words at all. What can we do? Let us say that if we can use this most profound idea of God, then we do not need to add to it the notion of existence, since that would make it a two-ness, having itself and existence as its parts. So if words limit the idea of God, then this God is beyond existence as well as beyond words that refer to anything existing, so that we should not even say that God is God, or use the term in any way. So, the word "beyond" carries much significance and in the end it is necessary not even to use the word God.

JESUS

I notice that you stress the word "idea" when you speak about the Good. While I may not understand why you stress the term, I do see that it is important for you to do so. My Greek is often called vulgar, or common, so you may be making a point I am not familiar with.

SOCRATES

Yes, there is often a bit of confusion about the idea of ideas. For a moment try this: if you were in a stream of water it is likely that you could describe the effect the water had on you, and also describe the water itself. It is the same for the most brilliant light of Being, the divine luminosity, since once having the experience one can say it was the most real of any experience, a beauty beyond all experiences of beauty, the state where you know it touches on Truth. In our Greek the term "idea" means "to behold." So, from "beholding" that experience one can say that these Ideas can be drawn from that experience.

Thus, these Ideas are also eternal and have a mode of existence beyond all those others. Given this we can say the Ideas of Reality, Beauty, and Truth are indeed ideas, but far different from the mere concepts that we call ideas, so we capitalize the word Idea to declare that we stress their difference from ideas that are merely concepts.

So, we can say there is a difference between having an experience of the Idea of the Good and the Good itself as much as there is a difference between the brilliance of sunlight and its source, the sun.

JESUS

Yes, beyond all else there is no term, but that even excludes the idea that God is nothing, doesn't it? For nothing is, after all, referring to something that is said to have no qualities, and that is not equivalent to something that surpasses all categories. Interesting that we share much. Surely, in one way, it is not surprising, and in another, it is.

Socrates

It looks like we both have entered the same stream of Wisdom. What would you say most clearly mirrors your own vision?

Jesus

You go to the heart of things and go there quickly. As they say, the nearer you are to the light, the more you are full of that light. Beyond that, they quickly add that in coming into that light one should be able to shine forth that light.

Socrates

Well said, Jesus. I would only add that how close one comes to that light depends upon one's ability and aptitude for receiving that gift of the divine. The coming into that light is a return as the departure is a procession. Together they are a whole moving in opposite directions both up and down.

Surely, the whole has both motions, as does all kinds of creation. It has a motion in and out of the gap. Apart from these motions that receive the new and release the old, there is something that always remains the same, persists unchanged, and steadfastly is what it is in an unchanging way. What is this? Some give it the name of substance without wondering if each moment is truly a new creation. Then the existence of this substance endures for only a moment, an instantaneous moment, and it would not be something that is continuously present through all time. Another thought, is there something behind the appearances that receives the appearances? I have heard some say it is like gold both because it can take on any form and because of its natural glowing nature.

Jesus

We are of one Mind and reflect upon it in the same way. Could we not say it in another way? I like to reflect upon it as the cause of the celestial order and of a true motion that never varies. For this is the cause of the transformation of all things capable of being transformed. The power of such a cause is as profound as what we say of God.

Socrates

Then this is what mirrors your own vision, does it not? I say that because it is good to talk the Truth about the divine as we are doing. The law of Truth requires those who know the same, say the same about the same. Knowing, then, the Truth we speak the same Truth.

Chorus

Now they need a perfect language to tell their lies. Tie that up with this talk about fantasy and you have another mess. You say cultivate fantasy and be a philosopher. What utter nonsense this is. No philosopher ever said anything worthwhile because words can't carry meaning any more than pigs can whistle or meatballs bounce.

Anti-Chorus

You can scream out loud as long as you want and it will change nothing. Why not try reviewing your fantasy and see if they have some connection with the problems you are facing in your everyday world? I thought you would, at least, mention the discussion on that transfiguration as the most brilliant light of Being, but not so. Then, the talk about God being beyond all predicates fell on deaf ears, didn't it? Why not wake up for a few minutes and try some of these practices that they have been describing? Put aside your hostility and give your mind a chance to see itself.

Jesus

You brought me back to our question. Good. I was taken away just in reflecting upon our friend, Dionysius the Areopagite. It is a simple thing to say, yet it has far-reaching implications as all truths do. I would prefer to ask you a question so that you see that in answering, you too will have reached the Truth.

Socrates

I couldn't wish for a better way of going, and I welcome it with the same spirit.

Jesus

Very true it is, Socrates. Now who among your followers has come closest in advancing this idea of yours?

Socrates

Let's look at Dionysius the Areopagite for his insight into theology. In showing all the descriptions of God are metaphors he showed he was a master of metaphors, a key trait of philosophers. He saw behind it all a Reality that can be expressed as the One, the Unified; he reflected on *ousia*, and the activity that has given birth to our Cosmos. He placed a high value on dreams but had not seen how to bring them into his system of theology.

Jesus

Yes, he has a theology and a philosophy, but you stress his theology. He joins those of us who naturally are drawn to thoughts about the divine and we can say he was also religious. It just might be best if we separate out these terms and make clear our passage from one to the other. I have followed a religious order that also speaks of the divine in terms of the divine, so that we also have a theology if you mean by theology the study of the divine.

SOCRATES

To single out theology is a simple thing to say, yet it is has far-reaching implications as all truths do. Before I explain myself, I would like to ask you a question about a key idea of religion. If we do this, it is likely we will have a common point of departure. So please consider my question: Which is better for me to say aloud to all. Shall I say, "I came prepared to accept whatever happens to me as I go on my way exploring ideas and seeking among my fellow men their way to Justice and Truth?" Or, shall I say, "I have come to save mankind through my own efforts and bring them to salvation?"

JESUS

You are trying to bridge our differences by expressing what you take to be my position. However, I would need to change your question. Consider this: Which then is better for me to say aloud to all, "I came prepared to suffer for the sins of man so that they can receive heavenly salvation" or, "I am prepared to go through whatever is necessary for the sake of those who are striving for their salvation?"

SOCRATES

Now, that was helpful, Jesus, thanks for that. In the first, it is a call to suffer for the sins of all mankind, while the second is clearly only for those who are awake and striving for their own salvation.

JESUS

The difference is like the rays of the sun rather than the dim light reflected from the moon. Now, you know that it is pleasing to me for all to know and hear of this since it will help mankind from falling into their folly and sin. Clearly, training the mind to reflect upon the highest and complete Knowledge is the way it can illuminate human life. The union of the two can be brought about only by turning the Mind upon itself to recognize that there is only one dynamic behind both.

SOCRATES

That dynamic is Intelligible and we call it the Logos, don't we? When our pure theological teachings become known, these vulgar misconceptions drop away, revealing our pure philosophy of the Mind. The dynamic goes forth while remaining unmoved, yet extending to all capable of receiving its beneficial goodness. The sum of all this we call symbolic theology, and it was, of course, Dionysius who gave birth to it.

JESUS

Yes, that is well said, Socrates. Now, let me turn the tables around on you and ask if our Dionysius is akin to your own philosophy. I will enjoy hearing what you will have to say, like those who are old friends sitting in the shade sharing stories of their youth together.

SOCRATES

It is my turn, you say, to speak of him who stands above all other men of learning and whose vision awoke the sleeping minds of many. Yes, those who fear that awakening discarded him, but for some, he still stands like a beacon of light to guide man's soul to that divine luminosity. How shall I begin? With praises? But what would reveal his vision? So, let me say that he brought forward a vision that above all else one should contemplate. He said simply enough that to learn to see the profound in the obvious is to turn the eye of the soul to the Mind. In that reversion one reaches a Knowledge beyond all knowledge by leaving the passing images to contemplating the divine itself by itself.

His interpretation of the language of the Bible transforms it through an understanding of our own method of allegorization and analogy. As if by magic, the text prepares the soul for a journey along that road that all who know have taken. As astonishing as his bold way is, it brings the soul from a primitive vision into our philosophy without demanding any abandonment of any loyalty to the Bible. The centerpiece of his work is to show that in any description of God one can find parallels in the absurd and audacious descriptions of man's folly.

Jesus

Now, Socrates, as much I love hearing praises for our philosopher, I do hope you will continue and explain more fully how he achieves his philosophical goal.

Socrates

You are right about that, for it is sometimes difficult to separate the two. His ability to achieve what he does stems primarily from his recognition that behind the order of Nature is the unseen things of God. The Logos can be glimpsed as a power underlying the whole and its parts as a vital force that brings perfection to each moment that is. For all that is visible is nothing but images reflecting the inexpressible power of the *ousia* that functions as the cause for all that is. Observing in this way, he shares with us the wonder and awe he experiences as life flowing into itself, yet never departing from itself. We can collect all the expressions of God that seem so offensive when taken literally and discover behind them what the soul needs to contemplate the divine. To go beyond the literal means to step into the way things function and that is the way of understanding. Surely, this is the key to the Gospel of Mark's insistence upon understanding rather than faith or belief.

Jesus

Now, Socrates, understanding awakens the spirit to realization. Dionysius brings us to see the many notions of God can all be understood on a higher and more profound level. He mentions so many I need not repeat them all; surely to depict God as asleep, drunk, suffering from hangovers, as having malicious anger, and his failure to keep sacred promises ought to be enough. Still, I do think we ought to mention those sayings in the Song of Solomon by using utterances befitting a certain class of prostitutes. We both see what Dionysius did with these scandalous remarks that depict God in shocking ways. He showed us how to shed the appearance to reveal a true hierarchical Reality.

Socrates

Yes, he made it possible for the many to recognize that Mind is a necessary companion to the life of the spirit.

Jesus

His every word rings true and brings my soul to see once again the Beauty and meaning behind words spun from one who knows. However, I wonder if you have answered my question: What is it about Dionysius' vision of philosophy that you consider most clearly mirrors your own philosophy?

Socrates

I will need to make a change in your question; then I can answer it. He is one of those who delve into the implications of what we have put forward. We lived what they reflect upon. We wrote nothing down of our teachings for our followers to ponder. Dionysius reveals our message. What he is doing is to present our philosophy as an aid for the memory of those who would benefit by entering our philosophy through the Mind. He challenges all who can read his writings to enter into that journey that Parmenides set for the music of the soul's sacred journey. He offers it as the true theological teaching about God that is beyond all predicates.

JESUS

Do I detect a bit of hesitancy about bringing forward an answer to my question?

SOCRATES

Yes, you are correct about that. I deeply admire what he has done. To show a rational structure to theology is to bring others to see that the Logos can be reflected in his theology. I should say that he has Hellenized his reader, but better yet, I would say he shows Hellenization is the same thing as entering into a higher sense of rationality. My hesitancy is about raising a serious objection to such a profound thinker.

What does it mean that he chose to disguise his writings to appear other than what he was? He chose to appear as a companion to Paul. He was said to be present at the crucifixion and was the author of a Platonic philosophy disguised as being consistent with Christianity and going beyond it.

JESUS

Let me put the question again, but with a slight change. Is his theology the same thing as a perfect model for philosophy, or does philosophy fulfill itself with his theology?

SOCRATES

What if his theology is the Platonic system whose roots are found in Proclus?

JESUS

Then he turned Christians into Platonic philosophers without their knowing it. What does that make him? He uses Platonic thought to convert believers into philosophers. No, that's not clear enough. He interprets Christian images and metaphors philosophically and in doing so, brings to followers a higher state of mind.

SOCRATES

Then the core beliefs are interpreted philosophically while giving the appearance of a loyalty to those core beliefs. It does appear we have identified a new member of the class of interpreters.

JESUS

Yes, we may have a new member. His works were finally judged pagan and rejected after analysis of his works showed they were written in the sixth century and not in the first. What does that do for philosophy?

SOCRATES

We can conclude one thing, and that is when it is possible to reject an interpretation that challenges the literal reading of core beliefs, then the loyalists to that literalness will reassert themselves and reject the philosophical interpretation. Another thing, since his works were rejected, should they not also reject those who he has influenced? Certainly, we know that Thomas Aquinas cites him well over a thousand times in his works. Then, too, based upon this principle, there should be other very distinguished thinkers who also should be rejected. What do you say to that?

JESUS

Your skill for controversy few can match. You are saying that just as there is a need for understanding and practicing some spiritual practice, or meditation, so the religious must be open to bringing into their system such practices. Sounds simple, I would say, except that you are really saying that to the degree the spiritual element in man surfaces, so he should be open to whatever spiritual instruction and practice that can meet his need.

SOCRATES

Obviously, the need is there. So if any religion lacks such understanding of the practices necessary for the soul's quest for union with the divine, they should be open to absorbing from spiritual systems what they themselves lack. He established the need for a hierarchy of ideas, and in so doing he found a place for the central ideas of philosophy, didn't he? Dionysius disguised himself as if he was a founder of Christian metaphysics and developed further the notion of using hierarchical order in his philosophy, so that he advanced our philosophy. However, he belongs to the class of those who prefer to present their ideas in a disguised form, and in doing that, he offers an alternative to the understanding of the core beliefs of the old system. He uses the new while appearing loyal to those core beliefs, all the while creating an alternative to the literal reading of the core beliefs.

JESUS

Yes, he is a new member to our order of interpreters; thanks for that. However, I would like you to unpack that notion that you just dropped into our talk. What is this idea of order?

SOCRATES

The hierarchy Dionysius established became the foundation for the ecclesiastical order of the clergy and this is also the basis for creating a hierarchy of souls. This is, of course, another example of finding in the many those divisions or classes that can make intelligible the underlying order so that the particular advantage of each can be brought forth. We find this again in the Platonic division of souls into classes, from the *Republic*. These can be arranged hierarchically into five classes. The cultivation of these classes enlightens us to the power that can be released and manifested throughout the cultivation and activity of each. The psychic movement of mankind through any of the lower classes or stages of the soul into the more advanced is through the cultivation of the soul to realize more fully the destiny of man.

Jesus

Your repeated reference to the destiny of man brings me to wonder if that means you accept the idea that the Soul is one even though it expresses itself as many among mankind. So let me ask you: Am I hearing that you are saying that there is a unity of the souls of man? Many believe that is a strange doctrine. Does it not suggest or mean that all the particular souls are really only one? I say this because it is sometimes called the unicity of Soul.

Socrates

You heard well and that is what many call the problem. It is possible to view it that way, but a better way is to say all human souls in their striving towards a spiritual fulfillment express the destiny of man. Equally, the Intellect, or the Intelligible, is said to also have a unicity and it is analogous to that of the unicity of the Soul. The unicity of the Intellect strives for union with the One itself, and as it does so, it partakes of the supreme union.

Jesus

We have done well except for one thing. I wonder if we made a slip in our approach to this problem of our interpreters. I do believe that we left out a very significant Christian philosopher.

Socrates

Please say more. If we left something out, we need to recover from our fall.

JESUS

Ficino was a priest, a canon of the Cathedral of Florence, whose vision included Dionysius the Areopagite, which brings me to wonder in which of our divisions he belongs. He is unlike the Gnostic John that we discussed because of the rather amazing dedication he had in translating and making commentaries on much of your Platonic tradition and on one of the letters of Paul. He found in Dionysius a bridge to your Plato that created a synthesis of the Platonic tradition and Christianity. In this, he shared a similarity to my Augustine since he found his way into Christianity through his study of Plotinus.

SOCRATES

You are right about that; we do need to add him to our study. As I recall he is the one who translated all of Plato's dialogues, Proclus, Plotinus, and even Dionysius' writings into Latin. Wait, I should mention that he also did a very good commentary on Plato's *Parmenides*.

JESUS

What effect did Ficino's way of being and his work have on Christian Europe?

SOCRATES

His assumption, common to the age, was that Dionysius the Areopagite, whose writings became the cornerstone of Christian metaphysics, were actually a work designed to appear as the follower of Paul; but in reality they were written by one of Proclus' students, all to mask Platonic philosophy under the cover of Christian images. Before this was known, Ficino's writings gave an authentic stamp to a philosophical confirmation of Christian doctrine, making possible the claim that to be a philosophical Christian is to be a Platonist and to be a Platonist is to be a Christian.

Jesus

You say, "to mask Platonic philosophy under the cover of Christian images." However, could you not say that he uncovered a philosophical depth inherent in those Christian images and, so, made visible what was there to be seen even though few could see that before he said it? Now, it does seem that since we both are familiar with Ficino, we can ask about your understanding of how Dionysius was able to uncover that depth inherent in Christianity so that Ficino could carry the torch into the Latin world. And, am I correct in saying that for all his vast insight and work, that he didn't place dreams as essential to philosophy?

Socrates

Yes, he was another of those who did not mention the importance of the study of dreams.

Jesus

Well, since we have seen how Ficino brought about the marriage of the demands of faith with the higher use of reason, which illuminates the soul with Truth, then with that union, we can find another class or division. He found the bridge between the two, so we can call this class the bridge builders. While we may sing him praises, he is no longer regarded as worthy of study and contemplation. As you know, he believed Dionysius' works were genuine and that Dionysius was a companion of Paul, so after the discovery, Ficino was cast aside.

Socrates

Your idea that Ficino can be regarded as a bridge builder leaves out the primary role that Ficino played out in his life. He built his thought upon one who was in disguise and only appeared to be loyal to the core beliefs of Christians and interpreted them in terms of the alternative system, Platonic philosophy.

Jesus

Good heavens! It appears we need another member of the family of interpreters. What shall we call him? You know him better than I do.

Socrates

First, I'd say he accepted a deceiver's teaching of the value of a tradition of a Platonic philosophy without realizing he was fooled. He passed on the writings of Hermetic philosophy, as well as translations and commentaries on Plato's dialogues, and did commentaries of Plato's *Parmenides*, but, of course, excluded the value of dream work. His work became a synthesis of two traditions until they were rejected.

Jesus

Now, that is good, but I still do not have a clear picture of where he fits into the class of interpreters.

Socrates

Let me try again. He is an interpreter who unwittingly Platonized Christian core beliefs and added to the new philosophical tradition a profound depth.

Jesus

I can go for that.

Socrates

Well, if it so be, so be it.

Chorus

When you have to build your case from a known falsifier, you have to admit you've got a problem. Your Dionysius the Areopagite was found to be a clever crook, that's all he is and was. His attempt to subvert the teachings is sufficient argument to dump him and his writings. Sure, he tried to bring about a Hellenization of the West and it was a good try, but it flopped. However, I should admit that I liked hearing about what was said about the Logos.

For the Logos did take on the flesh and became what we can believe in. It rings through me and I wonder why it is linked to this idea of perfection. Wait a minute. Don't smile! The idea of perfection is the weakness in this discussion. Why? Because there is no perfection here. Maybe in Heaven there is, but not among us. We face only mysteries and they can't be solved. Whatever you can dump that was of the mystery means it wasn't much of a mystery to begin with.

Anti-chorus

Well, there is a change. You liked what was said about the Logos, good. Take a look. Could it be that you are a member of one of these divisions they are talking about? If so, could it be that you can't hear or accept anything other than what you believe in? Did you know that in the most profound of principles there is the Logos? This Logos was with God, so it is divine, isn't it?

Socrates

I would like to hear more of your comparison of Dionysius with your Gnostic John, so please continue.

Jesus

That is fair. Dionysius is much like our friend, John the Gnostic writer, since he clearly rejects the Pauline doctrine that faith is sufficient for salvation. Paul says nothing about the conditions necessary for entering the Kingdom of God, which, of course, is basic and central to the Gospel of Mark. Mark offers understanding

as the way to prepare the mind for the breakthrough we call the
Kingdom of God.

SOCRATES

Indeed, there is that way to the Kingdom of God. It is direct and
simple. But I think we also need something like what Plato started
in his myth in the *Phaedrus*. Indeed, I am sure you know of it. It is
where he describes the journey of the soul to experience the other
side of Heaven. In the journey, there are stages along the way, but I
would have liked all the stages of enlightenment from a glimpse to
the final stages fully worked out.

JESUS

With that I agree. Interesting it is that before our talk, I encountered some Zen masters and they spoke about their use of the
Ox-Herding Pictures for that very thing. In each picture, there is a
beautiful and profound statement of the state of mind of the seeker,
what is encountered, and how it functions. Each one ends with a
suggestion of its sequel so that as a whole, it does represent the
spiritual life of man.

SOCRATES

No, I had not learned of their map of the spiritual journey of the
soul. I do think it is time that I meet with them to explore similar
questions that we have entertained in our discussion.

JESUS

Now that would be interesting to learn about. I am sure I would
enjoy learning about it. If you do go ahead, I believe you should call
it: "The Dialogue between Socrates and the Buddha." However, I
still wonder about the shortcoming that you found in Dionysius'
work and in Damascius. Or should we stop here?

Socrates

No, you are right to recall what they both ignored. In Damascius' *History of Philosophy*, he does appreciate the role of dreams, but not their interconnections with dreams and visions. Our Dionysius does not have a place for them within his theology.

Jesus

I would like to hear from you if you have had dreams that included divine illumination as their central feature. Now that I reflect a bit on this issue, I think I would like to know what road did you travel that brought you into philosophy? Did dreams play a role?

Socrates

You are among those few who know the right questions to probe into your subject. I do hope I can answer them to your satisfaction. Since Providence guides us, I am obliged to share with you a few things about my life. Early in my youth, I heard the repeated refrain that life is empty of meaning and all we face is war, death, and dishonor. The view that was held was that there is a war between Heaven and Earth, between good and evil that is unending, eternal. The conflict was not merely between these mighty cosmic forces, but it is played out in our very souls. If you join the forces of good over evil, you gain Heaven, with all the nonbelievers going on to Hell. Obviously, there was no place or role for meaning in this eternal conflict, and certainly, there is no escape. So the believers condemn all who oppose them. I had stayed with this early group since at the time there were no meaningful alternatives open to me.

Then I was drawn to music; I became interested and, later, enchanted with it. I found myself attracted to those musicians who were able to capture a beauty that moved my soul. Here was a creation alive and present in the moment only to disappear nearly as fast as it came into being. Here I could see that some musicians had reached out and were touched by something wondrous, and this they brought into being from somewhere unknown even to themselves. There, as I said to myself, must be something few want to acknowledge. Here was a beauty that I realized emerged from a structure that exhibited principles of harmony. Harmony I hoped was itself a reflection of some higher and truly existing order and intelligibility. Yes, it might be dimly perceived, but nonetheless it was there to be participated in. It was impossible to carry the music away, yet its beauty lingered on long after the last string was played. I knew then that since there is beautiful music, that beauty must foreshadow an intelligence to cultivate. There must be two intelligent forces, as I reasoned, one glimpsed through such music and another more profound waiting to be discovered.

These reflections were sufficient to end my kinship with my young friends. Finding no kinship with this group, I was open to seek other views more akin to what I had found through Beauty. Everything changed when I heard someone at the Agora mention something that seemed so very strange to me, yet it had an instant acceptance as something that must be true. A young woman whose voice rang with integrity and truth said it. She said, "The whole of God sees, thinks, and it is the whole that hears." I recall vividly that it caused me to turn about and wonder if I could carefully watch each thought, and each thing I say and hear. If so, I could discover what it was that was experiencing these things. Surely, after such questionings, I could easily see that what was doing these things was one and not a warring God that drives a terrible fury within one's soul. Awakened to learn more, I heard that Heraclitus had said, "Wisdom is one to know the intelligence by which all things are steered through all things."

This very notion of the One intrigued me, and when I heard that Parmenides was to visit Athens, I knew what course I must by all means follow. He came with Zeno and he led us through his idea through which all became clear to me. For what else was left for me than to see as he saw, to realize what he had brought us to see. His method was dialectic, and that was enough for me to realize that to know the Mind through the Mind is to realize its very source. As for dreams, they played a major role in my life, but they came after I learned about Parmenides.

JESUS

Did your Plato capture Parmenides' vision into the source and nature of all that is?

SOCRATES

He brought me to see that without the idea of the Self there can be no true philosophy by bringing me to see through the dialectic that what can be said of the One can also be said of the Self. With a singleness of vision he guided me to see how the One-Self functions as the most brilliant divine luminosity. He revealed through his dialectic that between any two moments there is a gap that reflects in its outpouring a divine providential nature whose source is the One-Self. He showed in a single stroke the wall of belief that harbors all those who believe in that shadow of reality they cling to as if real. A relief came over me when he showed that the dualism so many take as real is empty, since neither the One nor all that is other can ever touch one another. Indeed, he then put all that I had seen together in such a way that I could not assume anything else was true. This he did by way of a demonstration that showed it was necessary, if by its denial it alone could exist.

JESUS

Really, you have done and seen what very few have seen and you have brought it together following the Logos. Wondrous it is. It is good that we have come together and shared what it is that we are.

But now let me confirm in my own words a key part of what you have said. You saw and made the connection between the gap and its divine, timeless nature. Did that idea of the gap become a mean term for what you sought to understand? If these are Parmenides' hypotheses, would you state it once more, giving any additional insights that you had?

SOCRATES

He showed that it was only through negatives that one could understand the One being beyond all predicates. He brought me to see that the dynamic inherent in the experience of Beauty touches upon Truth and was Intelligible. Most interestingly, he then brought me to realize that in every instantaneous moment there is participation in and from that Reality from which all change occurs. I found here in this wondrous dialectic of Parmenides that the moment is a gap that reflects the providential nature of the divine. So the gap is that which is beyond time and is continuously unfolding that which must be as it is. He also showed that those views I had formerly been exposed to could be grasped simply as his fourth hypothesis. Now a relief came to me as I saw these forms or views were merely another view of the One, but it was not sufficient for me. Lastly, he showed that beneath this later view was a dualism where Heaven and Earth and all such opposites played out their dance without ever touching the other. I should add that he was able to show the way each of these assertions about the One could be denied.

JESUS

Then you made the connection between the gap and its timeless nature. Did that idea of the gap become a mean term for what you sought? If these are Parmenides' hypotheses, could you state it all again more fully?

Socrates

Yes, the insight into the gap stayed with me for a long time. I came to realize that the assumptions we make about time and motion and rest clearly presuppose the second hypothesis. With another step, I was able to see that this second hypothesis can be seen, in turn, as necessitating the categories of the first hypothesis. Stated simply on reflection, it can be seen that the idea of the One, pure Being, and the Soul form a triad and this threesome are the first three hypotheses. The idea of Being is the notion we have called *ousia*; it is the major idea in both the second and third hypotheses. Going over these ideas is a contemplation, and the more sincerely entered into the more it becomes the soul's preparation for vision. The other hypotheses are as I have noted.

Jesus

So your reflections created the conditions for your search and the search brought you to the practice of the Mind-coming-to-know-the-Mind. I like that because it is contemplation that begins and ends in a true philosophy, and it is that which culminates in vision. Notice that it includes all the ways the Mind communicates to us. I do enjoy the way you are bringing all that together into a unity, thanks.

Socrates

We did cover much ground and included many ideas and there are some we left out, didn't we? We will need to go back, review them, and see how they may fit into our hierarchy of philosophers. Are there any you think important to review that we failed to mention?

Jesus

Yes, there is another who we need to review. We have overlooked him. Reflecting in this way has brought to my mind another philosopher whose teacher was Hypatia, who joined the church and became a bishop. I do believe you have heard of him.

SOCRATES

Yes, the mere mention of her name brings delight into my heart. You must be thinking of Synesius the Alexandrian. Here is a truly remarkable philosopher who did a study of dreams. Are you familiar with that work?

JESUS

I learned he was one of those who became a part of the church while remaining one of yours. I know that Hypatia often visits around here and that she has joined the contemplative group high above Mount Athos. I wondered how Synesius was able to retain his hold on philosophy while fulfilling his role as a bishop.

SOCRATES

He was reported to have said he had accepted much of the teachings of the church when it did not violate what he found to be true. From what I learned, he said that if he was called to the priesthood he would declare before God and man that he would refuse to preach dogmas in which he didn't believe. He made it clear that even the idea of resurrection was to him nothing but a sacred and mysterious allegory.

JESUS

There is little doubt about his views, but did he make clear that he considered himself a philosopher?

SOCRATES

Yes, indeed, he said clearly that he didn't wish to be anything but a philosopher.

Jesus

He said it simply and directly. Would you recall for me what he said about the importance of dreams? He surely stands apart from the other philosophers if he makes dreams not only important, but also essential to the spiritual life. It is only recently that I learned about the direction he had taken in philosophy. For, as you know, I have been absorbed in my contemplations for a period of time and have not kept up with such things.

Socrates

He stressed that dreams are especially significant to those given to philosophy since they open one to enlightenment. For he found that it was through dreams one can reach the receptacle of Truth, pure, brilliant, and divine, and he added that it was through this kind of pursuit that one would be able to see the future.

Jesus

Very important words that he passed on and they need to be reintroduced to those who regard themselves as religious. Among the things that he covered, what would you say you especially learned about his teaching and practice?

Socrates

Yes, I did learn what I needed to discover because I wanted to follow those who have a kinship with dreams as they practice their philosophy. He held that in the continuous study of dreams, the imagination becomes conjoined with a profound understanding that awakens the divine character through which intuitive intelligence, the eye of the soul, can be approached and experienced. He echoed our own understanding that it is from God that the knowledge of dreams comes. He made it clear that the Gods were not independent floating beings but rather pure Intelligences.

Jesus

So he was one of those who saw that dreams are the essential part of the art of divination. I call that good. Did he really believe that it was through dreams that not only philosophers, but all mankind could be visited by pure Intelligence and by God?

Socrates

Yes, he was one of those who recognized that dreams come to us all and that they reveal a personal knowledge about our struggles we most desperately need to know. I should add that, like us, he held that it was entirely unnecessary to interpret dreams. Dreams can become visible from the depths of their obscurity through the kind of reflection that we both know is the passageway to the divine.

Jesus

What think you, where shall we place Synesius? Shall we say he is like Ficino and fits into that same class of interpreters?

Socrates

They have much in common, but Synesius was the first to highlight dreams and fit it into a Platonic metaphysics. When we consider his membership in the class of interpreters, we need to distinguish him from the others. In accepting the role of a Bishop within Christianity, he allowed himself to be identified with the tradition of believing in the core beliefs of the church while he kept their allegorical meaning to himself. He stressed dream work that had no relevance within the church's teachings. Thus, he disguised himself as a follower of the core beliefs of Christians and treated their core beliefs allegorically while retaining their philosophical meaning, and he followed the importance of dream work, which was at variance with church teachings. What name does this give him?

Jesus

As difficult as it might be to realize this, we must say he was different from Ficino in that he consciously chose to believe he was being consistent with the church's views when treating the core beliefs allegorically and within the Platonic tradition. What does that make Synesius but a disguiser of being a member of those who hold to the core beliefs by treating their core beliefs allegorically and pursuing Platonic philosophy and dream work privately?

Socrates

Before we put a name on Synesius should we not review the questions we have about him? Shall I go first with my questions and then you follow with yours? Surely, he could be named one of the most profound of Platonists and a Christian, and that raises a most interesting question. Can he be both?

Jesus

Can he preach the one and conceal his philosophy?

Socrates

What shall we call a Platonist who becomes a Christian bishop and tells all that he will never preach anything he knows to be false? Did believers know that he treated them as children who had not yet learned to treat their beliefs allegorically as he did with the story of the resurrection?

He joins the church of those who skinned alive his very profound Platonic teacher, Hypatia, for her heretical beliefs. Would those who seek his help benefit by knowing from which tradition the Wisdom flows that helps them? Clearly, he is a Platonist and while we could both wonder why he accepted the post of being a bishop and why he was offered it, that doesn't change his being what he is, a Platonist. We could say he has become an inner Platonist and an outward Christian. In moving from an Academy to the church-temple he went from an open free association of thinkers who practice contemplation, dialectic, dream work, and self-analysis to those bound by belief, whose lives are directed by priests who are hostile to non-believers.

Can a Platonist have an inner life different than his outward? Can he be meddling in another business that is not only different from his own, but opposed to those higher principles upon which he himself lives? If he assumes a post to lead others in the life of belief is he not taking a post to defend and support believer's belief in what he himself rejects? Has he, in accepting the post as a bishop, divided the efforts of his soul so that he has become the ruler of all the dead that lay in ignorance? Is he guiding his subjects to remain loyal to what he should free them from and appearing to believe what he has rejected? Has he become unjust when his efforts should always be to have managed his own life and ruled himself so that in becoming one out of many he has become just and beautiful? Is this the state that we both know as Wisdom, since to preserve that inner state takes a knowledge we call Wisdom? Then he has betrayed the principle of Justice, a principle that lies at the heart of what it is truly to be human and assumed a role antithetical to his own philosophical principles.

Jesus

You are a hard master, Socrates. You judge him to be a traitor to philosophy.

Socrates

If the name fits, then that's all we can say.

Jesus

And now we need a conclusion, don't we?

SOCRATES

Yes, there is a need to bring all these ideas and practices together into a unity. Is it likely you will play a role in that?

JESUS

It would be my pleasure to do that, Socrates. I see that brings together theology, contemplation, dialogue, dialectic, dream theory, and the practice of bringing the Mind to understand its function and operations. From that description you just made, I see we have added two new members to our interpreters. But, as for this philosophy, where is it going on now and who are those doing it? I certainly would like to know more about it.

SOCRATES

I have heard something that is going on down there, but I haven't met any of those who may be doing it. I think it won't be long before I meet these new philosophers. I'll wait until I learn more before I say more.

JESUS

You say, "new philosophers," and you appear cautious about saying more. Why is that, Socrates?

SOCRATES

Well, I will risk saying a few words. Consider what we have been saying about these interpreters of ours. Notice that they bring forth even interpreters of interpreters and so we have a whole string of them commenting on their priors and advancing some point that degenerates to even more interpretations. None of them are doing what we did. They comment on what we have said and write their commentaries. Shall we conclude that we have not brought into existence those like ourselves, but only interpreters? Shall we say the obvious, that both of our ways of being express our practice as a way of life? Have we been amiss in not stressing this obvious truth? Philosophy is in the hands of scholars, not philosophers. As interesting as those commentaries might be, they are a far cry from participating in living dialogues that explore Truth and Reality. Again, look at those who presently are called philosophers and you can see very quickly that they are lovers not of Wisdom, that clear and brilliant light of Being, but philodoxers, or lovers of opinion.

So I have heard that there is a breed of curious seekers who have not only been exploring dreams and contemplation, but they even write new dialogues taking off in a direction akin to ours yet different in an interesting way. They have revived Homer's midwifery and developed a method and practice to accompany it. So, yes, I am cautious about calling them a name because it is not clear, at least not yet, just where they are really going.

Jesus

Now, that is interesting. It suggests another member of the class of interpreters. Could they be members that continue the Platonic tradition and add significant elements to it? It seems they may even be those who live their life in conformity with their philosophy and have become exemplars of their philosophy.

Socrates

I do think you are right about their being a new member of the class. As I consider it I think that they may not be interpreters at all, but exponents of a living tradition.

This raises a question. Shall we consider that the divisions we have made are similar to psychological types of man? For in reviewing our divisions have we not identified certain attitudes, or states of mind, that block a more full participation in the spiritual life? There may be different ways of describing psychological types, but with our work we know that these divisions mark the degree that one can enter into the spiritual journey.

Jesus

Yes, you are right about that, but we need to place them in a hierarchical order. I would place Synesius on the top of our list, then Dionysius the Areopagite next in line. He showed that the metaphysics of both of our traditions can become one, and in that move, we can reconcile the other Abrahamic religions with the highest understanding and insights of our spiritual traditions. However, in terms of interpreters, we know that Synesius allowed himself to appear as a defender of the core beliefs of Christians, while treating them allegorically. Dionysius appeared as a Christian while presenting the core beliefs of Christians allegorically within a Platonic philosophy. Synesius held to the value of dreams, while not so with Dionysius. Neither made a public presentation of their fundamental views nor engaged in dialogues with their fellow man. Now, how would you rank the next in order?

Socrates

You are right placing Synesius as high as you do. As for Dionysius, while he does ignore the role of dreams, he was clearly a major player in both of our traditions.

Jesus

For the third place, I would put those loyalists that we mentioned, but they do have their narrow vision that keeps them from seeing the whole of which we recognize has the meaningful parts.

Socrates

What shall we say about the last? Shall we say they are those who deny and falsify our teachings and distort the truth they failed to see?

JESUS

I do think we should pause and wonder about that group you mentioned that is returning to your own vision and carrying it on to new levels, because we might be able to add them to our divisions.

SOCRATES

What is still in progress has yet to reach its fullest flowering. Surely, we should wait to see what emerges in all its fullness before we bother grading them and including them in our divisions. Another way of judging them will be to see what opposition comes forward, for that is often another way of judging significance, is it not?

These divisions do cause a set of problems and the bitter struggle between them is obvious. Or shall we say that any integration within oneself has its implications on those in opposition?

JESUS

Without seeing how it brings about changes among mankind, we cannot really judge the importance of each of our divisions. Each of these divisions actually represents stages of man's development and so they can be called different states of mind.

SOCRATES

Yes, it is true that there is and always has been a fear among those in the lower divisions towards those in the higher, and most so toward the highest. I don't think we can challenge that after seeing what we went through, can we?

JESUS

So you are stressing that what is behind man's struggles to flourish and survive is simply a struggle over what state of mind will flourish and which not. You understand all this as a kind of war for and against certain states of mind. The consequences of this struggle, you say, play themselves out within the family, city, and in the Cosmos itself.

Socrates

True, and add that each of these states of mind has an image that attracts some and repels others. The struggle between them underlies the structure of society and it plays itself out within each soul. Each of these players in these divisions finds ways to justify their positions and to vindicate their actions. As a result, there is a conflict or war between them as to which shall be the dominant image of man. As each gains and loses power, so society is transformed. With the introduction of a new idea, these forces align themselves for and against one another.

A new idea coming into society may upset the power structure and the stability of the life of many. With change comes the loss of the advantages that had been derived from understanding the old. Learning and mastering how to take advantage of such changes directly affects the positions of honor and power within systems of society and within the soul, for benefits are distributed accordingly to positions of power.

A sense of stability comes with identifying with a system, so that when challenged it may be defended furiously. Power holders always defend the status quo and chief among them are the oligarchs, or powerful moneyed interests. If a new idea gains power, it threatens the stability of power holders.

Jesus

The most ancient of truths are always new to those loyal to an interpretation of the old. Every interpretation is an attempt to save the old to preserve some advantage. What is new is often only new to those in whom their vision is blocked.

SOCRATES

Yes, and when the new idea offers a fundamental change in the power structure, the struggle becomes intense. When the new idea argues that its truth overcomes past privileges, then the struggle becomes a life-and-death issue. Behind it all is the fear of the Mind. The possibility that a rational order is superior to all other claims forces a re-examination of an entire culture.

JESUS

And it is true that behind all this drama and clash of ideas is the fear of the Mind and freedom. Further, when it is tied to awakening to a new kind of thinking, we know it will arouse the fear of the Mind. Behind that fear is that new forms of order and understanding demand a difficult retraining and adjustment.

SOCRATES

The pull to oppose the new and resist change is a fundamental conservative impulse, as looking forward to meaningful change is an opposite movement. The issue between these forces hinges on whether the proposals of each benefit the growth and development of the soul. When it can be demonstrated that only one is true and reflects a higher Truth, then the issues become critical.

In this struggle over Truth, it becomes necessary to say which of these comes closest to revealing and making Intelligible the Truth of the ideas being contested. Where can one confirm what we have explored through a process of reasoning through words and appealing to the kind of experience that comes along with an encounter with Intelligence?

When reasoning brings with it a quietness of the Mind and one can drop away everything to see what sees, it is then that sight opens itself up to itself, the Self. Equally, the drowning oneself in empty phrases breeds chaos.

Jesus

Yes to that, and much more needs to be said. Behind the fear of the Mind lies another threat that periodically sweeps across the land bringing death and destruction along with it. These are the times when the literalists gain power. They cannot stand higher truths beyond their reach nor do they have any desire to make up for their shortcomings. They believe they already have the truth and will destroy whatever stands in their way. When they seize control of any of these divisions, they reduce it to what they can understand and burn the rest.

They have been exposed only to the drama of belief and fear the perils of non-belief. They cannot stand to view what they take as true and subject it to analysis. They hold fast to their literal reading that supports their belief. Yet these beliefs are claims that need to be examined. Surely, there is only one standard to examine the truth of any spiritual and philosophical truth. Whatever claim is being made as true needs to be demonstrated by a reasoning reflection and confirmed in experience by those whose primary interest is the Love of Wisdom balanced by their experience of the Intelligence.

Jesus

True, and the way we have been exploring these ideas would be a good model for that very task. Our way of proceeding through these divisions has made the task simpler and clarified much as we went along.

Socrates

Well, we have seen how these divisions we have made break down to their corresponding ideas. Have we not seen that with the introduction of a new philosophical idea, we can find those who accept it as it is, those who reject it, those who offer alternative systems of belief to the teaching, and those who adapt the new to their own beliefs? Now, shall we call those who see a fundamental philosophical unity between the old and the new another division? These are the ones who could see behind the parables a Logos that unfolds the Intelligible. Actually then, we could say these divisions are phases of one search for meaning. The conclusions need to be verified in one's own experience and contemplated as the unfolding of the Logos.

Jesus

I have been careful to note just how many divisions we have found among our interpreters and if I am correct I do think that there are ten divisions in the class of interpreters. Would you agree to that number?

Socrates

Yes, I agree to that. Is it likely that these are all the possible members of that class? And would you say that this means that anytime a new idea comes into a society that already has a different or opposing set of ideas, that these are the ways interpreters will react to the new idea?

Jesus

I will have to gather them together and see how each relates to one another and to the whole. I just had an idea that I would like to ask you about. What would you say if someone came up to you and simply asked, "What is the mark of an interpretation?"

Socrates

Now, that is curious, because here we have been talking all this while about the different kinds of interpretation but we have not discussed what is the singular mark of interpretation. Perhaps we had to see its various forms before we could express its essential feature. Now, I would say that interpretation assumes that whatever is being interpreted cannot stand alone, nor be understood in itself, and this is the justification for interpretation.

Jesus

I will use your own way of reasoning to offer my view. First, Socrates, you use many words for describing the condition for an interpretation but fail to describe what it is. I would simply recall what we have said, and that is, whenever someone adds or subtracts from a work it is an act of interpretation.

Socrates

Well, you did it and did it right. Whoever cannot stay within the words of a work and adds or subtracts from it, then that is indeed an interpretation. What is needed, then, is after an interpretation the interpreters should return to the original text and show they have not departed from the meaning found in the text or spoken work. Or we can say, when these additions and subtractions are made, that means the original work must have been weak and needed interpretation to strengthen the work, or it was too wordy and needed some shortening or subtraction.

Jesus

However, if a work is complete and needs nothing to be added, or if nothing should be cut out, then it can stand alone as a challenge for readers or listeners to come to know it in itself and for itself. The difficulty might be that there are not that many works that meet this condition. Now, what name would you give for the kind of work that needs no interpretation?

Socrates

It would be self-sufficient, Intelligible, and worthy of challenging man to comprehend it in its own terms. I would call it a true and noble work.

Jesus

Not many cultures would be open to such noble works.

Socrates

Yes, if these ideas that we have discussed were unknown to a culture or society, they would experience difficulties introducing them into their society. We have covered much in our search and in doing it we have celebrated the philosophical life.

Jesus

Yes, our paths do meet in that unity that we celebrate as the culmination of the philosophical spiritual life. The life of the spirit is not without Mind, and Mind is not without its spiritual dimension; so that being one, we move as one towards the divine. The divine is the Intelligible embracing within itself all that it has been and leading towards its destiny. The quest began with an openness we can call pure ignorance and moves towards what we have yet to experience in all its finality.

Socrates

However, the final stage is not in the realm of experience since it transcends experience. Many cultures would reject this idea and consider it heretical.

Jesus

It pleases me that you added a thoughtful addition to my position, and this is likely to upset the many. But for all that I would be pleased to hear you discuss it further.

Socrates

Yes, there is a better explanation, but we seldom express it openly because it is met with such scorn when it is shared. Unless the audience has a high level of intelligence, it will likely be rejected.

JESUS

Now, I find that intriguing. Please share this idea of yours.

SOCRATES

As it is above, so it is below.

JESUS

Would you mind unpacking that expression?

SOCRATES

First, let us review the obvious. We need to understand why those who have experienced the most brilliant light of divine luminosity conclude that they have reached Truth. Further, these people seek to teach others how to reach that state. Some go on and create a teaching from what they take to be the meaning of the experience. The reason they believe they have reached the Truth is not only because they cannot imagine anything more real and more beautiful, but that their light experience changes everything in their life, and by contrast, their former way of living seems empty and wasteful.

If someone is in such a state, or had experienced it, what if they were asked, "Does every single experience have a cause?" If they could endure that question, what if they would accept another question, such as, "Are causes superior to their effects, and also have an independent and prior mode of being?" Would not that person have to conclude that peak experiences are always secondary to their causes?

JESUS

Certainly, that is true. I will have to dwell on that. You have made me wonder about the effects of peak experiences. I find it challenging, and I suspect this idea will have far-reaching consequences.

However, Socrates, I do believe the fundamental difference between our approaches rests to a large part on my belief in one God and your belief in many Gods. God alone is and is the Lord of all, and no ruler can be Lord nor can a ruler be deified. Our freedom lies in this principle. God is not to be sought anywhere but in the heart and soul of man. To find him within is the Kingdom of God. This difference separates us, and it can be shouted aloud that it is the fourth philosophy of our people. We are neither Sadducees, nor Pharisees, nor Essenes, but are the fourth people; we were called the Zealots. Now, let it be said that no matter how many similarities we may find between our doctrines, it is this difference that is impassable. I have heard you have a way of making the many appear as a one, and among the many you have a way of placing them in a hierarchy; however that may be, every hierarchy has many members, so it is still a manyness, not a one. I would like to hear from you your reasoning on this matter.

Socrates

No, the difference is in our idea of what we mean by the word God. In truth, we agree that there is a highest divine source; we agree that there was a model for the creation of the universe and you call it the Logos. You say the *Logos*, or the *word*, was in the beginning with God and that means creation needed the Logos as a model for creation. It must be eternal and unchanging; it must have vitality and a mode of Being. Each of these unchanging features can be personified since they have a mode of Being. We say that God the creator uses the *Logos* as a paradigm, or as a model, like you say. But, surely, if it has a mode of Being or existing eternally, it must have a cause, since all that exists must have a cause. The cause of the *Logos*, or paradigm, we call Cronos; however, by the same reasoning, it itself must have a cause and that we say is Uranus. These are what we call Gods, and they can be personified and celebrated. The ultimate cause of all that is we say is the One or the Good. Your followers recognize that, and so we are in agreement.

Jesus

Again, my friend, Socrates, you have expressed it well. It has given me another idea to consider and reflect upon. As interesting as that is, I would like to know the role of Gods in your life as a philosopher.

Socrates

For myself, I see the need to say that Beauty itself exists, and it has a vast power. The overwhelming experience of Beauty drives those who do catch a glimpse of her to do whatever they can to gain a more full and complete vision of her. As you know, Wisdom is the most beautiful of existents so that philosophers are called lovers of Wisdom. To pursue her, they need the arts linked with Apollo, since he represents the powers that perfect and convert those attracted to harmony to reach intellectual Truth and the light that luminously resides there. His symbols are music since harmony is most readily seen through her inspired creations. Hermes has from the earliest of times been called the supplier of philosophy and elevates those souls akin to him; but unless they include in their study the dialectic, the power of the Logos, they will utterly fail to achieve the passage from that brilliant light of Being to the Good itself. Thus, we can say that in my philosophical journey, I pay heed to Aphrodite, Apollo, and Hermes.

Jesus

Very beautifully said, but I still wonder if you believe they are Gods. I believe you will say that it is not likely in the way I think of God. I imagine for all that, you will say that they really represent forces or powers that be, and that they exist eternally, doing what they do. However, do they exist as Gods?

SOCRATES

Yes to that, Jesus. You have seen what we call the elements of theology, and our philosophy expresses that vision in a way that preserves its integrity and truth.

JESUS

I just saw something of interest to us, Socrates. We have been searching to understand the mystery of the nature and kinds of interpretation, and I do think I have come to a solution to our problem. We have identified many kinds of interpretation and named each of their kinds, and while that has been important to do, it fails to present them hierarchically, and especially identify which would be on top of them all and which at the lowest level of them all. I just saw the solution to our riddle.

SOCRATES

There you are basking in the glory of the answer and smiling away. Please share it before you lose it.

JESUS

Well, Socrates, it is not the kind of thing that you can lose or forget. Is it not true that what we have been calling your Hellenic philosophy, and my own teachings, are primarily about the nature of the Self, which is to understand that sacred source through the Logos? Yet, do we not also add the need for presenting a way to confirm what we have said is true?

SOCRATES

That is true, and if our work is complete and can stand alone, then it exists without the need for any interpretation. We must conclude that it is self-sufficient, complete, and Intelligible in itself. It would not need an interpretation beyond its own understanding of our elements of theology. However, if there were any weaknesses in our theology, then the correction would add to its explanation and not be an interpretation. When there are no longer any possible additions, it would be called a complete work.

Jesus

If a work needs an interpretation it is incomplete and needs something to be added, or ignored, or rejected. Our work does not need any interpretation. The lowest member of that tribe of interpreters would introduce their own pathologos into a work.

Socrates

Then we have finished our work. We have described all the kinds of interpretation and named them. We share much together, but there is something that sets us apart, and it is this that I still wish to discuss with you.

Jesus

No higher purpose can there be than to discuss what might separate us.

Socrates

Good it is that we can discuss this because I wonder if we have different views of the very nature of God. I wonder if your idea of God is a kind of spiritual force that guides certain people through history.

Jesus

The God I speak of is a creator God, a God of my people. Our God is necessary to overcome the power of evil that is spawned by the evil one, Satan.

SOCRATES

Then God and Satan are not only opposites, but distinct and separate from one another, yet having the power to be and do what they do. Do you also say that to contemplate evil or to act in an evil way is to act irrationally and in a totally unintelligible way?

JESUS

Indeed, to sin, or to miss the mark you are aiming for, is to act irrationally and against one's own spiritual goal. The Good does not share its attributes with evil because they are as different as they are opposites.

SOCRATES

Do we share in the truth that for a God to be a God he must be and remain in a perfect state? And, is not being in a perfect state such that goodness would be the essential mark of a God?

JESUS

Yes, you have said it rightly, we drink from the same cup and praise the same God.

SOCRATES

Then, we both say that God abides eternally in his own state, and in doing so preserves his nature. If so, then would you agree that since his nature is good, he will utter no falsehoods nor will he be active in an evil way?

JESUS

Yes, the God over all, Heaven and Earth, has a nature of unfathomable goodness.

SOCRATES

Then would such a God be at war if war is the abandonment of the intelligible?

Jesus

For you the intelligible befriends the Good, while for us it casts a deceptive shadow over all.

Socrates

However, must we not agree that Satan, as the personification of evil, would lack the ability to plan and act intelligently towards any good he desires because his actions cannot reflect what is good or intelligible? Could he even go ahead and marshal his forces and prepare for the coming battle between Good and evil if his plans are irrational and, so, worthless?

Jesus

So proud is Satan that he accepts moments of victory to satisfy his evil nature.

Socrates

What is it worth if the end is known to overcome those moments of victory? For, surely you agree that Satan's battle plans and actions must fail since they lack intelligibility.

Jesus

The depths of arrogance keep all from seeing the obvious.

Socrates

And, if Satan was vanquished in such a way, would he not come to know, in Good overcoming evil, that evil itself was annihilated and only Good exists?

Jesus

The evil of Satan moves across the Earth leaving destruction and misery in its wake, and its constant victory over good gives ample proof of its existence.

SOCRATES

Can what has been thoroughly defeated continue to exist?

JESUS

As long as the continuous war rages in the soul, it mirrors the cosmic war.

SOCRATES

If evil is only found in Man, in his deeds and thoughts, why not look for the cause where it springs up rather than in a war between Heaven and Earth?

JESUS

You seek to end the war within Mankind and that leaves its source untouched.

SOCRATES

Where will evil play itself out if it finds no home in the soul of Mankind?

JESUS

While Truth is silent before the mysteries of Man's existence, I can see why you say what you say.

SOCRATES

Our mysteries reveal truth, yours conceal it with piety.

JESUS

Your own people do not know the dreadful power of Satan nor his devious nature. His evil is so vast and pervasive that no thought of good, nor desire for good could emerge within his nature.

SOCRATES

But, Jesus, did we not agree that God, being in a perfect state, could not co-exist with evil or he would not be in a state that is pervasively good throughout? So, God could not clash without departing from his true nature of goodness. Equally, could Satan enter into the state of the goodness of God without becoming to that very degree good? Certainly mingling with the good would compromise his evil nature.

JESUS

You are very thoughtful with your choice of words and I do see where your thought will carry you. You would say that each would be in totally different states, having different natures, and so no battle could occur between them. So, with a stroke of reasoning you would banish the thought of the coming Armageddon.

SOCRATES

Yes, that is where reason bids me to go, and with her I follow the Logos.

JESUS

It is likely that what you think is true; it has the mark of the rational, but the very existence of evil triumphs over your reason. For, we know the existence and power of Satan in the form of Sophia, or her son Yaldabaoth, or Eve, or further back to Marduk since they all are personifications of all pervasive evil. So, you can say there should be no battle between Good and evil even though there is and will be.

SOCRATES

In your teachings what would count as the pinnacle example of evil among mankind?

Jesus

There are many signs of the pervasive power of evil over mankind, but the most unspeakable of evils before God and man is in the willful slaying of one of God's chosen, as the beheading of John the Baptist by Herod. And, Socrates, in your teachings what do you count as the worst, or evil among you and your people?

Socrates

I need to return to Achilles, the favored of Athena. He was of the Achaean tribe and we would count him as the most dreadful of men because his fury was the direct cause of the loss of many brave warriors and the needless loss of his friend, Patroclus.

Jesus

We can both shed tears over the loss of loved ones, and surely we realize at that moment so dear that evil plays out its destructive hand.

Socrates

As amazing as it must seem, Achilles finally realized that he had been playing out something he had not known he knew; he had been blindly following a model of his surrogate mother, Lord Phoenix, and that this most fundamental ignorance in his soul had borne his misery. After this realization he rejoined the battle of Troy in a staggeringly mindful state and became our greatest hero. For us Hellenes, Achilles, by using the mind to free the mind of its folly, became the model for reversing one's errors and faults.

Jesus

You share an astonishing story that leaves me seeing directly the truth of your tale. Then, without the wisdom of the Goddess Athena, he freed himself from sin and folly.

SOCRATES

Now we have developed his art into the way of the philosopher as midwife to free man of his folly and to guide his way through the study of dreams.

JESUS

A drop of rain does not make a storm.

SOCRATES

True enough, but his ideal shaped the soul and spirit of the Hellenes into a mindful people that has put all others to shame.

JESUS

We share a path to heaven while we differ on the road to follow on Earth.

SOCRATES

The destiny of man lies in the single path of the Hellenes, for all need the path we have walked; to know thyself is to be Hellenic.

JESUS

And, you Hellenes do not think our Abrahamic God to be a God.

SOCRATES

Nor do your people realize that in the soul of Man there is the healing power of the Logos that overcomes the pathologos, the sick image of the Self.

JESUS

Yes, you have uncovered a difference that we will need to reflect upon further. And I shall wonder if our future talks will benefit both those here and elsewhere. I am sure I will find that out when we meet again to discuss further the nature of the divine, the way of benevolent Providence, and the nature of the Self.

Chorus

The shouting is over. You can claim a victory or dismiss it with a wave of the hand, just like me. So it may be that under all my talk, you caught a true believer. I'm not and that's all. I separated myself from all that long ago. It is just that I am fond of certain parts of a past faith more than I realized. That's all. All this talk is just ways to destroy opinions that you don't agree with. What you call the Mind just doesn't have it. It is not possible that this puny little figure of a man can comprehend the heavens. The mind is simply incapable of the task you guys put on it. What really matters is stability and end of conflicts. End this war between ideas because there are no solutions to the riddles the mind sets before itself. Whenever you need to laugh, just remember what's been said. Imagine saying to others that man sins because he is enlightened.

Anti-Chorus

You did, however, come to see that there was an idea that you so held to as so significant that if it fell all else would fall. Clearly, it awakened an old memory of a former belief. You saw, did you not, that your own position makes you a member of those who are unaware that they believe in a position. What does that mean? It means that you are a loyalist to your own fundamental unsuspected beliefs. Perhaps that is another division.

I wonder what effect this play might have on those we watched shaking the dust off their feet as they entered this meadow in these rolling hills.

END

About the Author

*P*ierre Grimes *has developed*, to perhaps the highest level, the use of the Socratic dialectic for understanding the types of problems we face when we struggle to attain excellence in our lives. This purely rational method of pursuing questions uncovers false beliefs, traces them to their origins, and by helping us understand their roots and the influence on our lives, deflates their influence.

Pierre calls this Philosophical Midwifery, a term that comes from Plato's dialogue *Theaetetus*, where Socrates refers to his art as midwifery because he assists in the delivery of men who are pregnant with either true ideas or false beliefs. Socrates calls his midwifery an art because it is the application of a knowledge that benefits the subject, which is in this case, the Self. This idea of art is explored in Plato's *Ion* and in Book One of his *Republic*.

For Pierre, the exploration of the dialectic as a mode of psychotherapy began during his years of counseling alcoholics at a rehabilitation center. As a result of his explorations during this time, he authored two articles, "Alcibiades" and "Vinodorus," published in 1961 and 1964, both written as Socratic dialogues presenting this process as a mode of psychotherapy.

The Noetic Society was founded in 1976 for the study of dialogue and the exploration of dialectic, and Pierre began demonstrating and teaching Philosophical Midwifery. In 1988, Pierre created To Artemis: The Challenge to Know Thyself, a computer program designed to guide users through four hundred structured questions that were modeled as a dialogue for users to record their answers an they explored their own problems. *Philosophical Midwifery: A New Paradigm for Understanding Human Problems, with a Validation Study by Regina Uliana, PhD*, was published in 1998.

Pierre has been a student of Eastern thought for many years. He received his PhD in comparative philosophy from the American Academy of Asian Studies, a graduate school of the University of the Pacific. There he studied with Lama Tada, Gi Ming Shein, Haridas Chaudrai, and Alan Watts. It was Alan Watts, in his autobiography, *In My Own Way*, who called Pierre a "true Jnana yogi, one who achieves enlightenment by a purely intellectual means." After attending many Sesshins, and meditation retreats, Myzumi Roshi and Koryu Roshi confirmed Pierre's enlightenment.

In 1982, the Son (Zen) master Chong-An of the Chogye Buddhist order of Korea invited Pierre to join him in the creation of a center that would combine Buddhism and Platonic philosophy. This became Opening Mind Academy and part of Virtue Mountain Temple. Chong-An gave Pierre the name Hui-An, conferred on him the title of Master Dharma Teacher and he was sealed as Chong-An's Dharma Successor. Chong-An was later sealed as Myo-Bong, the Patriarchal Dharma Successor of Venerable Hye-Am, the 33rd patriarch from Lin Chi.

Pierre was a full-time philosophy instructor at Golden West College in Huntington Beach, CA for fifty years and was a professor of philosophy at the University of Philosophical Research and the Holmes Institute, the divinity school of the Church of Religious Science. He conducted week-long seminars at Esalen Institute for over twenty-five years, as well as many meditation/philosophical exploration retreats at various locations. He and other members of the Noetic Society have presented his work in the form of demonstrations as well as papers at many international conferences.

The philosophical counseling movement began with Pierre Grimes' publications on the dialectic as a mode of psychology in 1961. In 1978, he incorporated his philosophical midwife program under the Noetic Society. He is the founder and Board member of the American Philosophical Practitioners Association; its President, Lou Marinoff, PhD, has recognized Pierre as the founder of this new direction in philosophy.

Additional Works by Pierre Grimes

Is It All Relative? Costa Mesa, CA: Hyparxis Press, 1995.

Philosophical Midwifery: A New Paradigm for Understanding Human Problems, with a Validation Study by Regina Uliana, PhD. Costa Mesa, CA: Hyparxis Press, 1998. Reprinted in 2023, available on Amazon.

The Philosophical Path of Dreams and Daydreams. Lulu.com, 2007.

Five Philosophical Dialogues. Lulu.com 2009.

Philosophical Perspectives from Pierre Grimes and Opening Mind Writers. Lulu.com 2009.

8,000 Years of Wisdom, by Michelle Abadie and Mike Cast, including a contribution by Pierre Grimes, compiled and published in the UK, 2009.

Pocket Pierre. Co-authored with Cathy Wilson, 2012.

"Dreams, Philosophical Midwifery, Soul" in *The Beacon of Mind: Reason and Intuition in the Ancient and Modern World.* Andrea Blackie and John H. Spencer, eds. Param Media, 2015.

In process, soon to be published:

The Return of the Gods

The Way of the Logos (second edition)

To Artemis: The Challenge to Know Thyself (adapted from the 1988 computer program)

Bibliography

The following works have influenced my writing of this dialogue:

Chief among them is the most excellent work of Burton Mack:

Mack, Burton L. *The Lost Gospel: The Book of Q and Christian Origins.* San Francisco: Harper San Francisco Press, 1993.

My New Testament Studies drew heavily from:

Aland, Kurt, ed., *Synopsis for the Four Gospels.* United Bible Societies, 1982.

Balboa, Juan and Maria, *The Logos According to John.* Juan and Maria Balboa, tr. (See Noetic Society website: noeticsociety.org).

Meyers, Marvin W., tr. *The Secret Teachings of Jesus: The Four Gnostic Gospels.* Random House, 1984.

The background of thought of Christian origins drew from:

Kloppenborg, John S. *Excavating Q: The History and Setting of the Sayings Gospel.* Minneapolis: Fortress Press, 1990.

Kloppenborg, John S. *The Formation of Q: Trajectories in Ancient Wisdom Collections (Studies in Antiquity & Christianity).* Philadelphia: Augsburg Fortress Press, 1987.

Kloppenborg, John S., Stephen J. Patterson, and Michael G. Steinhause., *Q Thomas Reader*, Sonoma, California: Polebridge Press, 1990.

Koester, Helmut. *Ancient Christian Gospels: Their History and Development.* Harrisburg, Pennsylvania: Trinity Press International, 1990.

O'Meara, Dominic J., ed. *Neo-Platonism and Christian Thought*, Albany, NY: State University of New York Press, 1982.

My study of the Presocratics was drawn from:

Wheelwright, Philip, ed. *The Presocratics.* New York, NY: Odyssey Press/Bobb-Merrill Educational Publishing, 1996.

The Study of Nag Hammadi texts drew from:

Meyer, Marvin W., ed., and Richard Smith. *Ancient Christian Magic: Coptic Texts of Ritual Power.* Princeton, NJ: Princeton University Press, 1999.

Sabar, Ariel. "*The Holy Land, The Search for Jesus, Unearthing the World of Jesus,*" *Smithsonian*, January/February 2016, Volume 46, Number 9, pp. 42–55.

Another most excellent work is Hathaway's:

Hathaway, Ronald F. *Hierarchy and Definition of the Order in the Letters of Pseudo-Dionysius.* The Hague: Martinus Nijhoff, 1999.

The central idea of Christianity is drawn from Bultmann's study:

Rudolf Bultmann, Rudolf, Bartsch, Hans Werner, and Reginald H. Fuller, eds., "Rudolph Bultmann's New Testament and Mythology: The Task of Demythologizing the New Testament Proclamation," in *Kerygma and Myth, A Theological Debate.*

London: S.P.C.K. (the Society for Promoting Christian Knowledge), 1953.

My readings of Plotinus drew from Juan and Maria Balboa's translations of Plotinus:

Balboa, Juan and Maria, *Plotinus.* Juan and Maria Balboa, tr. (See Noetic Society website: noeticsociety.org).

The works of Plato mentioned came principally from:

Plato: The Loeb Library Series, Loeb Classical Library Series, 2002.

The new translation of the important 15th Century philosopher Ficino was drawn from:

Ficino, Marsilio, James Hankins, ed., Michael J.B. Allen, tr. *Platonic Theology, Volumes* 3, 4, 5. Cambridge, MA: Harvard University Press, The I Tatti Renaissance Library, 2003–2005.

My insights into dreams have been influenced by Synesios:

Balboa, Juan and Maria, *On Dreams by Synesios.* (See Noetic Society website: noeticsociety.org).

The source of Neoplatonic thought goes back to:

Albranassiadi, Polymnia, ed. and tr. *Damascius: The History of Philosophy.* Lysimakhos, 1983.

Morrow, Glenn R. and John M. Dillon. *Proclus' Commentary on Plato's Parmenides.* Princeton, NJ: Princeton University Press, 1987.

Runia, David T. and Michael Share, trans., *Proclus: Commentary on Plato's Timaeus.* Cambridge, UK: Cambridge University Press, 2014.

The following is a selection of my published articles:

Grimes, Pierre, "Alcibiades: A Dialogue Utilizing the Dialectic as a Mode of Psychotherapy for Alcoholism," Yale University (QJSA) Volume 22, Number 2, pp. 277–297, June 1961.

Grimes, Pierre, "Vinodorus: A Dialogue Exploring a Frame of Reference for Dialectic as a Mode of Psychotherappy in the Treatment of Alcoholism," Rutgers University (QSA) Volume 27, Number 4, pp. 693–716, 1966.

Grimes, Pierre, "Contrasting Excellence in Homer with Philosophical Midwifery," *Philosophical Practice*, Volume 1, Number 1, March 2005, page 17.

Grimes, Pierre, "A Review of Some Philosophical Papers at the First Prometheus Trust Conference" (Book Review), *Philosophical Practice*, Volume 2, Number 3, November, 2006, page 195.

Grimes, Pierre, "The Betrayal of Philosophy: Rediscovering the Self in Plato's Parmenides," *Philosophical Practice*, Volume 11, Number 2, July 2016, page 1752.

Grimes, Pierre, "The Philosophy of the Self," *Philosophical Practice*, Volume 11, Number 3, November, 2016, page 1844.

Grimes, Pierre, "Philosophical Counseling and Philosophy," *Philosophical Practice*, Volume 12, Number 1, March 2017, page 1858.

Grimes, Pierre, "The Philosophy of the Self: The Logos and the Pathologos in Philosophical Midwifery," *Philosophical Practice*, Volume 13, Number 1, March, 2018, page 2063.

Grimes, Pierre, "Philosophical Midwifery and the Platonic Tradition," *Philosophical Practice*, Volume 15, Number 1, March 2020, page 2442.

www.ingramcontent.com/pod-product-compliance
Lightning Source LLC
Chambersburg PA
CBHW071457140726
47997CB00005B/1761